To my parents.
I never would have gotten this far without you.

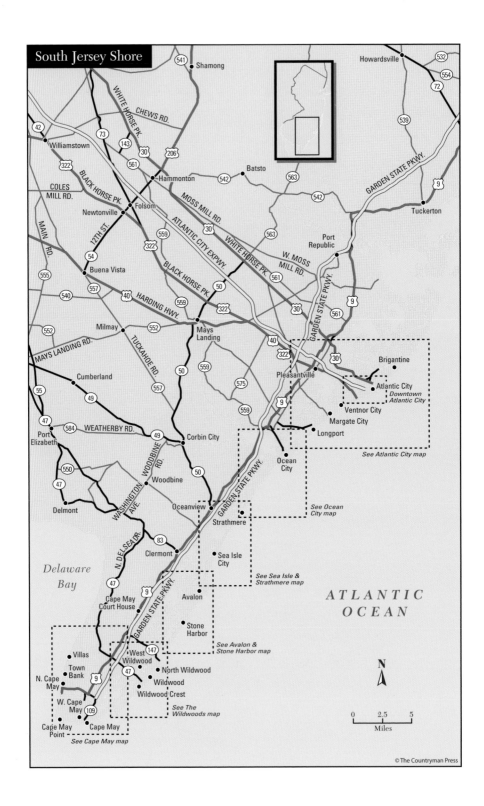

South Jersey Shore

541 Shamong
532 Howardsville
554
72
42
73 143
Williamstown
CHEWS RD.
539
WHITE HORSE PK.
30 206
561
322
COLES MILL RD.
BLACK HORSE PK.
Hammonton
542
Batsto
563
GARDEN STATE PKWY.
9 Tuckerton
Newtonville
Folsom
MOSS MILL RD.
542
12TH ST.
MAIN RD.
ATLANTIC CITY EXPWY.
30
WHITE HORSE PK.
563
Port Republic
559
322
54
Buena Vista
BLACK HORSE PK.
50
W. MOSS MILL RD.
561
9
555
557
540
40
HARDING HWY.
559
322
30
561
9
552
Milmay
552
559
40
Brigantine
Mays Landing
322
30
MAYS LANDING RD.
TUCKAHOE RD.
50
559
575
Pleasantville
Atlantic City
Downtown Atlantic City
55
Cumberland
557
Ventnor City
49
559
9
Margate City
47
584
WEATHERBY RD.
49
Corbin City
Longport
Port Elizabeth
WOODBINE RD.
Ocean City
See Atlantic City map
550
GARDEN STATE PKWY.
47
50
Woodbine
See Ocean City map
Delmont
WASHINGTON AVE.
Oceanview
Strathmere
83
N. DEL SEA DR.
Clermont
Sea Isle City
See Sea Isle & Strathmere map

Delaware Bay

47
9
Cape May Court House
Avalon
GARDEN STATE PKWY.
Stone Harbor
See Avalon & Stone Harbor map

ATLANTIC OCEAN

Villas
West Wildwood
147
Town Bank
9
47
North Wildwood
N. Cape May
Wildwood
W. Cape May
109
Wildwood Crest
See The Wildwoods map
Cape May Point
Cape May
See Cape May map

N

0   2.5   5
Miles

© The Countryman Press

The Jersey Shore

The Jersey Shore

Atlantic City to Cape May

A Great Destination

Jen A. Miller

THE COUNTRYMAN PRESS

The Countryman Press ✳ Woodstock, Vermont

Explorer's Guide The Jersey Shore: Atlantic City to Cape May: A Great Destination
ISBN 978-1-58157-134-9

Interior photographs by the author unless otherwise specified
Maps by James Miller, © The Countryman Press
Book design by Joanna Bodenweber
Composition by Eugenie S. Delaney

Published by The Countryman Press, P.O. Box 748, Woodstock, VT 05091
Distributed by W. W. Norton & Company, Inc., 500 Fifth Avenue, New York, NY 10110
Printed in the United States of America

10 9 8 7 6 5 4 3 2 1

Contents

Acknowledgments

THIS BOOK IS the culmination of four years of work, from the day I started the first edition, through three years of article researching and writing, right up to Spring 2011, when I put the finishing touches on the chapters you're about to read.

I never, ever could have done this without a gaggle of people who gave me their time, their ideas, and their support.

Thank you thank you thank you to Michael Bruckler, Maureen Siman, Elaine Zamansky, and the entire Atlantic City Convention and Visitors Authority team for all your help, from giving me a big-picture view to verifying the tiniest of details. Thanks to you guys, we will all know the correct price of a ride on the Jitney.

In Ocean City: Michele and Jay Gillian, and Laurie Howie—thank you for telling me what I always needed to know. Special thanks to the ladies of Sun Rose Words & Music, not only for your ideas, but for supporting local authors and local books.

To the Catanoso clan: Marlene, Lenny, and Justin. My family wouldn't be the same without yours. Thank you for the wonderful summers in Avalon Campground, and your support throughout the span that it took to put two books together.

Jack Morey, Ben Rose, and Chuck Schumann—Wildwood would not be the same without you. Thank you for telling and showing me why. Special thank you to Amy Z. Quinn for her wonderful essay on Wildwood that appears in this book, and for putting into words what I never could about a place so many people love.

Jack Wright, Alicia and Victor Grasso, Terry O'Brien, Bob and Linda Steenrod, Jay and Mary Ann Gorrick, and Curtis Bashaw: Thank you for showing me why Cape May is one of the greatest places in the world.

A big thank-you to everyone who gave me photographs for this book: Justin Gaynor for the beautiful cover; Scott Neumyer, Chris Barrett, and

Mark Chesner for running out and grabbing shots for me as I closed in on my deadline. Also thanks to historians Emil Salvini, Ben Miller, Douglas Hunsberger, and James T. Hoffman for allowing me to tap their treasure troves of historical photos. Special thanks to Marc Steiner, whose photos you'll see throughout. I never would have learned so much about the entire Jersey Shore without you. Thank you for not fleeing when you realized what exactly went into saltwater taffy.

Special thanks to my research assistant, Brittany Wehner, for making all those phone calls and ensuring that this book is as accurate as possible.

To my good friends for listening to me in those final months, weeks, and days as I put this project together, whether it was allowing me to vent about the writing process, or just offering free dinner and a beer: Jen Gertel, Caren Chesler, Kristen Graham, Garrick Goh, and Bobb Hawkey. I couldn't have gotten through those final days without your support.

And to my family, for always being there for me.

Introduction

SO YOU'VE DECIDED to go down the shore—but you're not going to the beach or even to the shore. When you travel to the southern coast of New Jersey, you're going "down the shore," where within 45 miles you can find everything from casinos to gourmet dining to relaxed seaside communities, all with pristine beaches. Your Jersey Shore vacation is what you make of it, and I'm here to show you your options. There are a lot—trust me. I've been writing about the shore for years, and I'm still surprised by what I find.

HISTORY

The shore area was first inhabited by Native Americans, then by farmers who let their animals graze on the land. Fishermen soon followed and set up small towns along the water.

The South Jersey Shore as we know it today would not have existed without Philadelphia or its steamy summers. In 1790, Philadelphia was America's largest city, and living conditions weren't ideal, especially in summer, when temperatures could reach past 100 degrees with soul-sucking humidity.

In the 1850s, railroads started bringing people to the coast, and by 1880 a new rail line opened between Philadelphia and Atlantic City. Vacationers soon followed, and they kept going all the way south to Cape May. Congress Hall opened there in 1816. Few in town believed it would succeed—why would that many people ever want to stay in their corner of the world? Townspeople even nicknamed the building "Tommy's Folly" after Thomas Hughes, who built the hotel that is still standing today and the cornerstone of a busy shore town.

By the 1950s, going down the shore was a tradition for families from the Philadelphia area, and the subtle differences among the towns still hold

LEFT: Promenade in Sea Isle City

today. Ocean City was the family-friendly spot (no alcohol allowed, even as BYO); Sea Isle City, Avalon, and Stone Harbor were the quieter towns with a preppy appeal and jeans-and-T-shirt casual bar scenes; Wildwood was where the action was without the gambling. It was even known as Little Las Vegas since Vegas performers, including the Rat Pack, flocked to the Wildwoods when the heat turned up too high in the desert. Many Victorian buildings in Cape May had been destined for demolition, but a push by local citizens in the 1960s and 1970s saved her gems and started a townwide redevelopment kick that eventually swung up to the Wildwoods—where folks work to save their Doo Wop motels as opposed to gingerbread cottages.

What you'll find today is a shore in its prime. People have realized the value of shore homes, and real estate prices now match. Where you could maybe buy a lot or two for $20,000 in the 1960s (as my grandfather had the opportunity to do), it's not uncommon these days to see for-sale prices that cross the $10 million range—though there are plenty of more affordable options.

Even changing real estate hasn't stopped vacationers from coming down to enjoy the sights, the sounds, and the water. If you're reading this book, you're probably one of them. Whether you found the shore by accident, or you've been coming here since you were a baby, there's plenty of new things (or new-to-you things) to see and do down the shore.

TRANSPORTATION

If you're coming from the Philadelphia area, you're probably driving down via the Atlantic City Expressway, accessible through Rt. 76 in Philadelphia, then Rt. 42 in New Jersey, which feeds into the Atlantic City Expressway. If you're headed to points south of Atlantic City, you can hop onto the Garden State Parkway (exit 7S), which ends in Cape May.

If you're coming from New York, make your way to the Garden State Parkway and ride it south through the state (getting on the Atlantic City Expressway if that's your final destination).

These highways can be

Surf fishing in Stone Harbor   Courtesy of Stone Harbor

Wildwood boardwalk   Courtesy of Mark W. Chesner

extremely crowded and congested in-season, especially on weekends. Many people have found back roads around the mess, usually via Rt. 55. But there are more back-road routes than grains of sand on the beaches—too many to reprint here. They're a combination of small-town and country roads, and can make for excellent sightseeing.

Atlantic City has an international airport. It's small, serviced by Spirit and AirTran. Most travelers reach the region via the Philadelphia International Airport. Many of the casinos run bus transportation from Philadelphia, or you can take the New Jersey Transit train into Atlantic City.

New Jersey Transit runs bus service through the Jersey Shore, but it's not always efficient. You'll have better luck with in-town transit systems, like the Atlantic City Jitney and Cape May Trolleys.

How to Use This Book

IF I WERE TO WRITE about every place to eat, stay, and play down the shore, you'd be reading an encyclopedia. So instead I've written a selective guide and recommended what I believe are the absolute best of the best, from budget-friendly to beyond luxurious, from romantic to family-friendly. It's a guide to help you make your experience a fantastic one.

You can also read updates about the South Jersey Shore on my blog at downtheshorewithjen.com, or follow me on Twitter at twitter.com/jersey shorejen.

ORGANIZATION

This book is organized geographically along the southern part of New Jersey's coast, north to south, starting in Atlantic City and ending in Cape May. I've separated each chapter by island—the Atlantic City chapter includes Ventnor City, Margate, and Longport, for instance, and Avalon and Stone Harbor are grouped together. I've also included select highlights of nearby inland towns. The chapters are then organized per what you'd be looking for—lodging, dining, recreation, culture, and shopping. You'll find everything in that category, no matter where on the island it may be, in that chapter. The end of each chapter also includes weekly and annual special events, plus further information you might need, including emergency numbers and contact information for Realtors in towns where most of the available lodging is private residence rentals.

PRICES

Everything at the shore changes all the time, so I've created price ranges for lodging, dining, recreation, and culture. These prices reflect the ranges that you will find at the height of tourist season—in many spots, the prices for

House of Blues at the Showboat   Courtesy of Caesars

lodging are much lower in the shoulder and off-seasons. Weekends and holidays usually carry extra fees in-season, too. Sales tax in New Jersey is 7 percent.

Price Codes

Code	Lodging	Restaurants (per entrée) and attractions (per adult)
$	up to $75	up to $10
$$	$76–150	$11–25
$$$	$151–250	$26–40
$$$$	more than $250	more than $40

SEASONS

For the purpose of this book, *in-season* refers to late May–early September; *off-season* means everything else. These dates reflect the unofficial beginning of summer—the dates surrounding Memorial Day weekend—and its end, Labor Day weekend. But every spot has a different idea of what in-season means, so these are approximations only. I've tried to mark when hours shift in the off-season, but this is something that can change each year, or even each week. You're best served by calling ahead of time if you're visiting outside holiday weekends. Most smaller places in Ocean City, Sea Isle City, Avalon, Stone Harbor, and the Wildwoods are closed in fall, winter, and spring, but Atlantic City and Cape May maintain almost full operations year-round.

mia

GEORGES PERRIER
CHRIS SCARDUZIO

Atlantic City

THE ORIGINAL SEASIDE RESORT

Including Ventnor City, Margate, Longport, and Brigantine

HISTORY

ATLANTIC CITY was a pile of sand when Thomas Budd bought the island for four cents an acre in 1695. By 1877, it had become the getaway spot for working-class Philadelphians, nudged along by $1.25 round-trip train tickets and promises of sea air as a medical cure-all. For a pittance, city workers left the hot, humid city for the shore, which became known as Philadelphia's lungs. Hotels, housing, restaurants, concert halls, and amusements soon followed.

By the turn of the 20th century, Atlantic City was the destination vacation spot, and not just because of the ocean. It was a release valve, whether that release came from seeing three first-run movies in one day on a Boardwalk pier or from one of Atlantic City's less legal draws: booze, broads, and backroom gambling. Drinking was never really illegal in Atlantic City, and town officials and shop owners violated Prohibition laws. It kept the city flush. Even World War II helped Atlantic City. Its hotels were turned into hospitals and housing for soldiers, and Boardwalk Hall, which usually hosted conventions and the Miss America pageant, was used as grounds for soldier exercises.

But Atlantic City started to slide in the late 1940s when the soldiers came home. Technology gave it a hard shove in the wrong direction. The benefits that would pull people out of the cities could suddenly be had at home. People moved to the suburbs, installed air-conditioning and swimming pools. Just like you didn't need to go to Atlantic City to drink, you weren't limited by train routes to one destination. You could drive farther

LEFT: Mia   Courtesy of Caesars

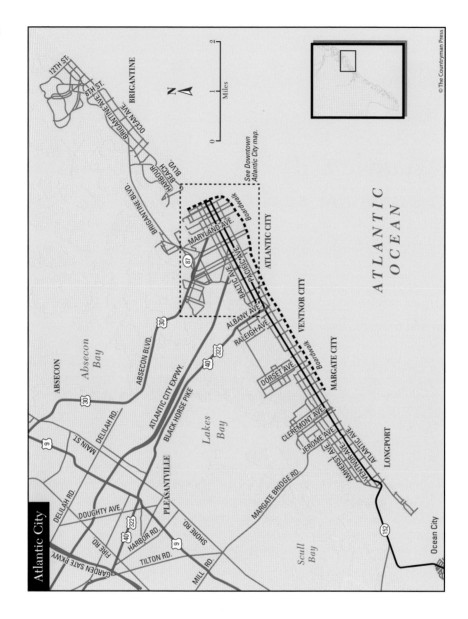

© The Countryman Press

south on the brand-new Garden State Parkway to younger and fresher Wildwood. You didn't even need to *drive*. You could fly to Florida without bankrupting your family.

Atlantic City collapsed. The once grand hotels shut down, or were turned into housing for the poor and elderly. Crime took hold, and not the benevolent-dictator, kickback kind that ruled the city in the 1920s. The middle class fled inland, leaving a shell of a resort town behind.

Of the solutions put on the table to right Atlantic City, gambling—regulated gambling this time—stuck, and was made legal in Atlantic City in 1976. Resorts, created inside the old Haddon-Chalfonte Hotel, opened in 1978. People waited hours to get inside.

Gambling has given the town a boost, but it has also brought its own demons, like crime, gambling addiction, and poverty, which is why, even today, some parts of Atlantic City are not safe at night.

When it comes to gambling towns, Atlantic City has long played second fiddle to Las Vegas, and not without reason. It's much smaller, with limited room for expansion. It didn't help the town's reputation that many visitors were senior citizens brought in on bus tours. That image started shifting in 2003 when Steve Wynn, who is credited with starting the luxury casino trend in Las Vegas, opened the Borgata in Atlantic City. This 43-story casino hotel set out to woo the young, hip, rich, and cash-paying crowd back to Atlantic City—people who didn't expect a free room in exchange for gambling.

The Borgata   Courtesy of Borgata Hotel Casino & Spa

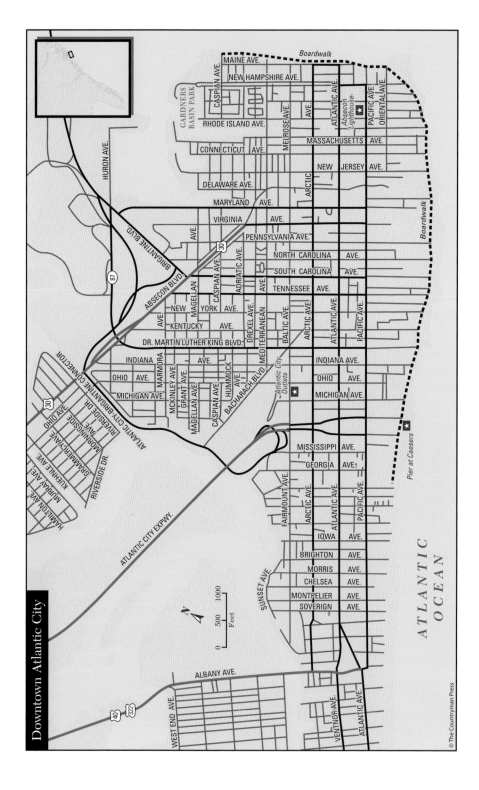

Downtown Atlantic City

© The Countryman Press

Atlantic City beach Courtesy of Atlantic City Convention and Visitors Authority

The Borgata kicked off a renovation and redevelopment trend. Almost every casino has spruced itself up. Resorts, Harrah's, and Trump Taj Mahal added new towers. The Chelsea, a glittering boutique hotel without gaming, opened in 2008. ACES, a new train line, runs directly from New York City to Atlantic City on weekends. The goal of these developments is to make Atlantic City more than just a gambling town and return the resort crown to the original playground by the sea. It's worked in part, though gambling revenues have been crippled by new slots parlors in Pennsylvania and New York. Some of the older casinos that didn't step up and reinvent themselves are in bankruptcy and might even be closed by the time you're reading this book. ACES now runs in season only. The state of New Jersey had to help finance final construction of Revel, a megacasino now set to open in June 2012.

As of press time, the governor of New Jersey had announced a plan for the state to take over the Boardwalk and marina casino districts in Atlantic City. For updates on the final legislation, and what it means to Atlantic City, go to pressofatlanticcity.com.

Today you'll find that the two sides of Atlantic City—the historic seaside town and the gambling mecca—coexist. Most of the flash and glitz is contained in the Boardwalk and marina areas. Restaurants range from pizzerias and ice cream parlors to luxury dining. And of course there's the beach, which is one of the few in southern New Jersey that doesn't require a beach tag.

Atlantic City is neighbored by Brigantine to the north and Ventnor City,

CAPT. YOUNG'S RESIDENCE AT NIGHT, MILLION DOLLAR PIER, ATLANTIC CITY, N.J.

Color postcard (probably hand-colored photo) of Capt. Young's Residence At Night, Million Dollar Pier, Atlantic City; circa 1913–1916.

Margate, and Longport to the south. These towns are more typical of the sleepier, family-friendly shore spots you'll read about later in the book. The lodging is more B&Bs and inns, or you can rent a home for a week.

Combined, Atlantic City and her neighbors make for an interesting visit. Within a 10-mile span, you can fly high on a parasail, nosh on gourmet fare, go all in at the power table, gawk at Tiffany's diamonds, nap on the beach, and tour a 65-foot wooden elephant.

An elephant? Read on.

Pick Your Spot

Best places to stay in and around Atlantic City

Borgata Resort & Spa Hotel Casino (866-692-6742; theborgata .com),1 Borgata Way, Atlantic City 08401. It's the newest casino hotel in Atlantic City (until Revel opens in June 2012) and caters to the affluent crowd looking for a city-like experience down the shore. You can pick a room in the original Borgata tower, or the new Water Club tower. Either way, expect top-of-the-line luxury. $$$–$$$$.

Caesars Atlantic City Hotel Casino (800-443-0104; caesars ac.com), 2100 Pacific Ave., Atlantic City 08401. Hail Caesar! This ancient-Rome-themed casino is located at the center of the Atlantic

The Chelsea Courtesy of the Chelsea

City Boardwalk. It has four towers of rooms—Ocean Tower's were recently renovated and redecorated into suites. Lucky for you the rooms are more Tuscan villa than ancient Italian conqueror. Don't skip a walk through the lobby, even if you're not staying. $$$–$$$$.

The Chelsea (800-548-3030; thechelsea-ac.com), 111 S. Chelsea Ave., Atlantic City 08401. The Chelsea made a big splash when it opened in Atlantic City in 2008. It's a boutique hotel that presented a nice place to stay without the noise and smoke of the gambling floor, all in an upscale setting. Think 1950s retro chic that would work as a set in *White Christmas*. You can book rooms in one of two sections: Cheaper, smaller rooms are in the Annex, while the nicest are in the Tower. In

The Boardwalk

Atlantic City is a spot of many firsts: first picture postcard, first beach patrol, first use of the word *airport*. But its best-known export is boardwalk.

The Boardwalk (always a capital *B* in Atlantic City) wasn't built as a way for tourists to walk along the beach, or as a pathway to 47 blocks of casinos, restaurants, and shops. It was born out of frustration. Alexander Boardman (get it? *Board* walk), a conductor of the Camden & Atlantic Railroad, was fed up with tourists bringing the beach with them into his railcars. So, using wooden planks, he made a collapsible footpath prototype. His idea was a hit with hotel owners—they didn't like sand in their lobbies, either. In 1870 the city built a 10-foot-wide boardwalk 1.5 feet off the sand. It wasn't a continuous, permanent fixture as it is today. That Boardwalk was made of 12-foot-long sections that could be picked up and moved in storms and winter.

The Boardwalk was so successful that it became a tourist attraction

James Salt Water Taffy on the Boardwalk

early 2010 owner Curtis Bashaw said he was open to turning the Chelsea into a boutique gambling hotel, though no decision had been made as of press time. $$–$$$$.

Come Wright Inn (609-822-1927; comewrightinn.com), 5003 Ventnor Ave., Ventnor City 08406. Stephen and Dianne Wright make their house your home—literally. The couple lived in this Victorian home for more than a decade before converting it into a six-bedroom B&B. All proceeds go to the church across the street, the Way of Life Assembly of God (the Wrights are missionaries). That doesn't mean the hotel is lacking in any of the conveniences you'd expect from a B&B. It's been meticulously renovated and maintained to reflect its turn-of-the-

A mile of the Atlantic City boardwalk. Wikimedia Commons; public domain

itself, and still is, year-round. Today it's more than 4 miles long and the hub of activity in Atlantic City. It's the easiest way to get to and from most of Atlantic City's casinos, with lots of restaurant and shops and bars along the way.

At the South Jersey Shore, you'll find boardwalks in Ocean City, Sea Isle City, Avalon, Wildwood, and Cape May, though those in Sea Isle City and Cape May are made of concrete. And you'll find imitators all over the country, from California to Hershey Park to Florida. But Atlantic City's Boardwalk is still the only one to carry the capital *B*.

century heritage. If you're looking for space, the two-bedroom Rossing Suite is your best bet. The largest accommodation in the inn, it features excellent views of the ocean as well as a private sitting room. If you're traveling by yourself, the Huntsford Room is one of the few single-occupancy places in the area. $$–$$$.

Harrah's Atlantic City (800-2-HARRAH; harrahs.com), 777 Harrah's Blvd., Atlantic City 08401. Harrah's is one of the three casinos not on the Boardwalk strip. Rather, it's tucked along the bay with the Borgata and Trump Marina. The newest addition is the Bayview Tower—which, you guessed it, offers views of Absecon Bay. The latest and greatest thing to do here is to visit the Pool at Harrah's, which is 86,000 gallons of relaxation for adults only. The areas around the pool are used for events, and it becomes a nightclub in the after hours. $$–$$$$.

Irish Pub Inn (609-344-9063; theirishpub.com), 164 St. James Place at the Boardwalk, Atlantic City 08401. The inn is a cozy, comfy, and budget-friendly Victorian spot in Atlantic City. It's more like some European accommodations in that guests share a shower. For those who are a little more reserved, rooms with private showers are also available. They offer single-occupancy rooms, too, if you're flying solo. $–$$.

Sheraton Atlantic City (609-344-3535; sheraton.com/Atlantic City), 2 Convention Blvd., Atlantic City 08401. The Sheraton is primarily a business hotel—there's no casino—since it's attached to the Atlantic City Convention Center. It's an ideal place to stay if you want to be a bit removed from Atlantic City's gambling scene, though it's close enough to the action that you can walk there. The Sheraton is also home to the Miss America memorabilia—dresses and shoes from pageant contestants are on display on both floors of the grand foyer. $$–$$$.

Trump's Taj Mahal Casino Resort (800-825-8888; trump taj.com), 1000 Boardwalk at Virginia Ave., Atlantic City 08401. India meets Atlantic City at this prong of Trump's Atlantic City

Harrah's Atlantic City   Courtesy of Caesars

Atlantic City Pet Hotel and Grooming

(609-348-8660; atlanticcitypethotelandgrooming.com), 547 N. Trenton Ave., Atlantic City 08401. Atlantic City isn't the most pet-friendly place in New Jersey (pets aren't allowed on the beaches, on the Boardwalk, or in most hotels), but you can still bring your cat, dog, or even parrot along for the ride. Take them to Atlantic City Pet Hotel and Grooming, which was started by Jackie and Scott Winston after they were thrown out of their room because of Jackie's service dog. None of the animals here is caged, and the dogs are walked—individually, not in groups— several times a day. Shuttle service for the pets is provided to and from Atlantic City hotels, and you can pick up or drop off your animals 24 hours a day. Resorts Casino Hotel just added a pet program in spring 2011. Call 609-344-6000 for more information.

empire. It's a big one, too. The building has 4.5 times more steel than the Eiffel Tower. If you've got money to burn, check out the Alexander the Great Suite: 4,500 square feet, including a sauna, weight room, bar, lounge, and pantry. $$–$$$$.

Local Flavors

Taste of the town—local restaurants, cafés, bars, bistros, etc.

2825 (609-344-6913), 2825 Atlantic Ave., Atlantic City 08401. This nook of a restaurant only seats 48, which keeps it an intimate fine-dining experience, especially given that owner Joe Lautato, or a member of his family, greets guests every night of the week. Reservations are a must—and even those can be hard to come by unless you know someone. Dinner. Closed Sun.–Mon. $$$.

Adam Good Deli (609-344-6699; adamgooddeli.com), the Tropicana, 2821 Boardwalk, Atlantic City 08401. Quick service, hearty servings, and low prices make Adam Good Deli a damn good bet. It's close to the Boardwalk entrance to the Tropicana if you want to stop in for a midday meal. Breakfast, lunch, dinner. $.

Angelo's Fairmount Tavern (609-344-2439; angelosfairmount tavern.com), 2300 Fairmount Ave., Atlantic City 08401. There's no fuss or muss at this corner tavern, but the food is excellent and served in larger-than-life portions. The menu is, of course, Italian and has plenty of seafood, pasta, and fried items. For the full experience, ask to taste their homemade wine. Want to give

Historic Smithville

In the 1700s, Smithville was a stop for stagecoaches traveling between Leeds Point and Camden. When railroads replaced stagecoaches as the preferred method of travel, travel routes and travelers migrated to nearby Brigantine. By the 20th century, Smithville had all but ceased to serve travelers, and many of the buildings showed it.

In 1951, Fred and Ethel Noyes, antiques dealers from Absecon, bought one of those crumbling buildings for $3,500 and turned it into a restaurant and inn, reopening in 1952 as the Colonial Inn at Historic Smithville. They started buying historic 18th- and 19th-century homes from all over the South Jersey area and moved them to the site that would become Historic Smithville. Today, those buildings are filled with shops and restaurants.

The shops come in all stripes, from kitchen to fashion to toy stores. And even if Smithville was created around the idea of America's past, it embraces many cultures through festivals and shops in town. In October, for example, Smithville is host to both an Oktoberfest and an Irish Festival.

a great gift to someone coming to AC? They do gift certificates. Lunch, dinner. $$.

Annette's Restaurant (609-822-8366), 104 N. Dorset Ave., Ventnor City 08406. This little brick-front restaurant looks like your mom's kitchen, and the food is as good and filling as a home-cooked meal. Eat at one of the benches or in the middle of the room at what looks like—you guessed it—Mom's kitchen table. It's loud like a family reunion. If it's too noisy, try to grab one of the outdoor tables. Breakfast, lunch. $.

Atlantic City Bar & Grill (609-348-8080; acbarandgrill.com), 1219 Pacific Ave., Atlantic City 08401. This favorite-with-the-locals hang-out has become less of an unknown gem, but who can blame visitors for wanting to chow down on the rib or crab platters? Expect a party atmosphere in the later hours. Lunch, dinner, late night. $–$$.

Back Bay Ale House (609-449-0006; backbayalehouse.com), 800 N. New Hampshire Ave., Atlantic City 08203. What better way to celebrate a good day than by toasting sunset? The folks at the Back Bay Ale House do so every day the sun is shining and setting. If you're in the mood for fries, go for the Old Bay variety. The spice, traditionally used for crab dishes, makes all the difference. Breakfast, lunch, and dinner in-season. Call for off-season hours. $$.

Beach Bar at Trump Plaza (800-677-7378; trumpplaza.com), Trump Plaza Hotel & Casino, Mississippi Ave. at the Boardwalk, Atlantic City 08401. You might expect just appetizers at this beach bar, which was voted one of the 21 sexiest beach bars in the world by the Travel Channel, but they also dish up salads, pizzas, and a raw bar. Still, the main attraction is the drink menu, which is loaded with what you'd need a blender to make: margaritas, daiquiris, coladas, plus

Boardwalk Empire

In 2010 HBO gave Atlantic City the star treatment through *Boardwalk Empire*, a glitzy drama series about Atlantic City during Prohibition staring Steve Buscemi and helmed by Martin Scorsese. The show is based on a book of the same name by Nelson Johnson, an Atlantic County judge.

"Prohibition was clearly the zenith of Atlantic City," says Johnson. The book is a history of the island that focuses on three political bosses—Louis "the Commodore" Kuehnle, Nucky Johnson (no relation), and Frank "Hap" Farley—who made sure Atlantic City was the place to indulge yourself without punishment.

"Atlantic City flaunted the law for a very long time and got away with it because of their political connections," Johnson continues. "Morally, intellectually, emotionally, it was no big deal."

While Scorsese took some artistic liberties with the truth—and doesn't hide that he has fictionalized the world in Nelson's book—the show is worth checking out on either HBO or DVD.

Crowded Boardwalk, Atlantic City, N. J.

island-themed drinks. Lunch and dinner in-season. $–$$.

Bobby Chez (609-487-1922; bobbychezcrabcakes.com), 8007 Ventnor Ave., Margate 08402. No need to go out on a boat for fresh seafood. Bobby Chez offers gourmet seafood dishes, like jumbo lump crabcakes, broiled crabcakes, lobster mashed potatoes, and coconut shrimp, as carry-out entrées. Just reheat at home. Expect long lines on holidays. Open 11:30 AM–7:30 PM Fri.–Sat., 11–7 Wed.–Sun. $$.

Bobby Flay Steak (866-692-6742; bobbyflaysteak.com), Borgata Resort & Spa Hotel Casino, 1 Borgata Way, Atlantic City 08401. Celebrity chef Bobby Flay opened his first steak house at the Borgata. Architect David Rockwell, who's designed Broadway sets, renovated FAO Schwarz in New York, and created a Cirque du Soleil theater, engineered the dining space, which is light and airy given the heavy presence of wood and glass. Steak takes the spotlight here, but don't skimp on dessert. The banana split is divine. Dinner. $$$$.

Buddakan (609-674-0100; buddakanac.com), Pier at Caesars, 1 Atlantic Ocean, Atlantic City 08401. This is the third Buddakan restaurant from restaurateur Stephen Starr (the original is in Philadelphia, the second in New York City). A trip to Buddakan is much more than just a sumptuous, modern

Buddakan   Courtesy of Caesars

meal. It's a dining experience, set in the dim, cool dining room where you eat under the gaze of a big golden Buddha. Lunch, dinner. $$$.

Capriccio (800-336-6378; resortsac.com), Resorts Atlantic City, 1133 Boardwalk, Atlantic City 08401. Capriccio has one of the best views of any restaurant in Atlantic City—its terrace offers both Boardwalk and ocean views for ample people- and beach-watching. That's not to detract from the food, which is gourmet northern and southern Italian dishes. The Sunday brunch is a treat and, at a fixed price, a smart splurge. Reservations recommended. Closed Mon.–Tue. Dinner, Sunday brunch. $$–$$$$.

Casel's Supermarket (609-823-2741; casels.com), 8008 Ventnor Ave., Margate 08402. While most big grocery stores down the shore are inland, Casel's is blocks from the beach and has free parking for customers. Expect all the brands you know and love, plus a deli, a bakery, and an assortment of beach items like pails, Wiffle ball bats, and boogie boards. Open 8 AM–10 PM Mon.–Fri., from 7 AM Sat., 7 AM–8 PM Sun. in-season. Call for off-season hours. $–$$.

Chef Vola's (609-345-2022), 111 S. Albion Pl., Atlantic City 08104. This restaurant, which has been dishing up Italian cuisine in Atlantic City for almost 90 years, is a local favorite, and a Zagat favorite, too—they rated it one of

Restaurant Hours

If you're wondering why so many AC restaurants are open only a few nights a week, check where they're located. Many casino restaurants will close for a night or two during the week because the casino offers so many other restaurant options.

the best restaurants on the Jersey Shore. No credit cards. Reservations required. BYOB. Dinner. Closed Mon. $$.

Cuba Libre Restaurant & Rum Bar (609-348-6700; cuba librerestaurant.com), Quarter at the Tropicana, 2801 Pacific Ave., Atlantic City 08401. Step back into 1950s Havana at Cuba Libre, which is both restaurant and bar. The food is, of course, Cuban, which carries influences of Spanish, African, Creole, and Asian cuisines. In keeping with Cuban tradition, the bar leans toward rum-infused drinks and even has its own brand of rums. In summer don't be surprised to find Latin dancing and DJs at night, and Latin floor shows. Lunch, dinner. Late night Fri.–Sat. $$–$$$.

Custard's Last Stand (609-823-4033), 107 N. Dorset Ave., Ventnor City 08406. For a sweet treat post-meal, or something to cool you off in the middle of the day, Custard's dishes up custard, milk shakes, smoothies, and sundaes. Eat inside in the air-conditioning at or one of the many shaded tables outdoors. Open noon–midnight Sun.–Fri.; till 1 AM Sat. in-season. $.

Dizzy Dolphin (609-347-7111; hiltonac.com/dining/dizzy-dolphin), 3400 Pacific Ave., Atlantic City 08401. I say the following in the nicest way possible: This is a ridiculous bar. It's a ship set just inside the entrance to the Atlantic City Hilton as you come in off the Boardwalk. You will make a joke about the *Titanic* "Jack, I'm flying!" scene. And that's okay. It's hidden treasures like this that make Atlantic City fun to explore. I have always stopped here for a drink before dining at the Knife & Fork Inn. $–$$.

Dock's Oyster House (609-345-0092; docksoysterhouse.com), 2405 Atlantic Ave., Atlantic City 08401. Dock's Oyster House has been a local favorite almost since the founding of the town. Harry "Dock" Dougherty opened the place in 1897. It's still family owned and operated, now by Frank Dougherty, who also runs the Knife & Fork Inn. As you can imagine, there's a lot of fresh seafood at Dock's, and their wine list has been recognized with an award of excellence by *Wine Spectator*. For a bit of history, choose from "Dock's Classics"—recipes and dishes, like crabmeat au gratin, lobster tail, and fried oysters, that have been on the menu since 1897. Dinner. $$$.

Downbeach Deli (609-823-7310; downbeachdeli.net), 8

Rolling Carts

If that walk to the next casino seems like too long a trip, hop in a rolling cart. Don't worry—it's not considered uncouth. Rolling carts have been around almost as long as the Boardwalk. The drivers wait all over the Boardwalk and at every casino exit. Plenty cluster around the Pier at Caesars, too, if you need a ride after shopping and/or dining.

S. Essex Ave., Margate 08402. Eat in or take out, kosher or non-kosher, Downbeach Deli has all the options. It's also the closest thing you'll get to a diner in Margate. They're known for their omelet menu and monster sandwiches. If you're going for lunch, don't skip the hot peppers they put on the table. Unusual? Yes. Delicious? Definitely. Breakfast, lunch, plus dinner until 10 PM. $.

Dune (609-487-7450; dune restaurant.com), 9510 Ventnor Ave., Margate 08402. *The Philadelphia Inquirer* praised Dune as serving "easily some of the most sophisticated food down the Shore." The setting is vintage beach with old woodwork and black-and-white photographs decorating the walls. The menu—which changes daily—offers twists on restaurant staples. BYOB. Dinner.

Boogie Nights at Resorts   Courtesy of Photographics by Tom Briglia

Club Life

If you're looking to party it up in Atlantic City, the town that's "always turned on" has plenty of nightclub options. The music is loud and pumping, and most of the clubs have in-house dancers. What's hot and what's not changes quickly in Atlantic City. For the latest, click through atlanticcityweekly.com. They have a free iPhone app of bars and restaurants, too, which you can download from their site or the iTunes store.

Boogie Nights (609-340-7698; resortsac.com), Resorts Atlantic City, 1133 Boardwalk, Atlantic City 08401.

C5 (800-548-3030; thechelsea-ac.com), the Chelsea, 111 S. Chelsea Ave., Atlantic City 08401.

Casbah (609-449-1000; casbahclub.com), Trump Taj Mahal, 1000 Boardwalk at Virginia Ave., Atlantic City 08401.

Mixx (609-317-1000; theborgata.com), Borgata Resort & Spa Hotel Casino, 1 Borgata Way, Atlantic City 08401.

mur.mur (609-317-1000; theborgata.com), Borgata Resort & Spa Hotel Casino, 1 Borgata Way, Atlantic City 08401.

The Pool at Harrah's (800-2-HARRAH; harrahs.com), Harrah's Atlantic City, 777 Harrah's Blvd., Atlantic City 08108.

Providence (609-345-7800; providenceclubac.com), Quarter at the Tropicana, 2801 Pacific Ave., Atlantic City 08401.

Closed Mon., as well as late Dec.–Apr. $$$.

Flying Cloud Café (609-345-8222; acflyingcloud.com), 800 New Hampshire Ave., Atlantic City 08203. This casual restaurant has a simple menu that leans heavily on seafood, which makes sense: It's located literally on a dock, and (weather permitting) you can eat dockside at their outdoor bar and grill. Even if you're inside, the view is superb. Aside from being surrounded by ocean, owners Ross and Mary Anne Constantino have decorated the interior ceilings with baseball caps from around the world. Lunch, dinner in-season. Closed Jan.–Mar. Call for off-season hours. $$.

Irish Pub (609-344-9063; theirishpub.com), 164 Saint James Pl., Atlantic City 08401. I hit the Irish Pub on a weeknight in summer, noshed on some pub grub, and chatted with a father–son pair who'd lost a bundle that day at the poker table. It's that kind of bar—the kind where you can talk to strangers over food and a pint, and one of the homier places in Atlantic City. If you're looking for a full meal, the Irish Pub is more than willing to accommodate, though the bar is a major draw. Lunch, dinner. $.

Johnny's Café and Bakery (609-822-1789; johnnyscafeventnor.com), 9407 Ventnor Ave., Ventnor City 08406. All the cooking and baking are done on site at this Italian restaurant, which has a casual and laid-back vibe. Don't overlook the baked goods; owner John Liccio owned a bakery before turning this Ventnor City spot into a restaurant. Breakfast, lunch, dinner. $$.

Knife & Fork Inn (609-344-1133; knifeandforkinn.com),

Renault and Prohibition

Renault Winery is the longest continually operating vineyard in the United States. They started putting out their products in 1870 and haven't stopped since. But how could that be when prohibition took wine off the shelves for 14 years?

Through a shift in product and some genius marketing: Renault obtained a permit to keep making wine for religious and medicinal purposes. The religious wine went to the churches. The medicinal product was Renault Wine Tonic, which was supposed to soothe an ailing stomach. It also had an alcohol content of 22 percent (compared to the 9 to 14 percent that's typical of today's wines) and a label warning that if the tonic was chilled, it would turn into wine, which led to rather than detracted from sales. Atlantic City even had "nurses" giving one-glass doses to Boardwalk patrons.

Bathers escape the heat on the Atlantic City beach. Courtesy of Jen A. Miller

Atlantic and Pacific Ave., Atlantic City 08401. The Knife & Fork has a history as colorful as Atlantic City itself. Opened in 1912, it's survived two family feuds, two shutdowns, and two renovations to remain as an upscale restaurant right off the Boardwalk. In its latest incarnation under Frank Dougherty, who also owns Dock's Oyster House, the Knife & Fork offers an extensive surf-and-turf menu that uses local ingredients, from the seafood in your entrée to the tomatoes in your salad. The Knife & Fork also offers more than 1,000 wines and a full bar. If you're not in the mood for a big sit-down meal, you can eat on the "porch"—an enclosed lounge with TVs. Reservations recommended. Dinner. $$$$.

Laguna Grill & Martini Bar (609-266-7731, ext. 102; laguna grill.com), 1400 Ocean Ave., Brigantine Beach 08201. This beachside eatery is almost two different restaurants in one. The deck is ultra-casual—feel free to have a drink while still in your bathing suit. Dinner is a different story. You won't need a jacket, but flip-flops and tank tops are out. Their specialties are the filet and crabcake surf-and-turf. Don't miss out on the *martini* part of the name—the menu includes 25 varieties. For a sweet treat, try the Creamsickle martini, a grown-up version of a childhood classic. Breakfast, lunch, dinner. Deck: $$. Dining room: $$$.

Los Amigos (609-344-2293; losamigosrest.com), 1926 Atlantic

Boardwalk Hall

(609-348-7000; boardwalkhall.com), 2301 Boardwalk, Atlantic City
08401. Boardwalk Hall might look like just another big concert hall if
you're here to see one of the knockout acts it hosts, like Bruce Springsteen, Jimmy Buffett, Bon Jovi, and Lady Gaga. But when what was
then called Convention Hall opened in 1929, it was a marvel of modern architecture. Situated on 7 acres of concrete and coming in at a
then unheard-of $15 million price tag,
Convention Hall was the largest audito-
rium in the world to be built without
posts or pillars. The 137-foot arched
roof with 10 steel trusses was
designed to hold itself in place, allowing unparalleled and unobstructed
views of whatever was happening
onstage.

Convention Hall was also home to the world's largest pipe organ, a
Midmer-Losh Company instrument that had more than 33,000 pipes.
The building's ballroom had another, smaller organ built by the W. W.
Kimball Company.

Boardwalk Hall has seen musicals, boxing, the Harlem Globetrot-
ters, ice hockey, indoor football, polo, bowling, Ice Capades, bike
races, Judy Garland, horse shows, and, of course, Miss America,
which first sent the most beautiful woman in the country—at least for
that year—down the runway in 1933 and again in 1940. It wasn't until
1946 that the organization attached itself to the building as its home,
then it left for Las Vegas in 2006. It's also the only place the Beatles
have ever played in Atlantic City (they were taken out of the building
by laundry truck to avoid 19,000 screaming fans).

In 1998 Boardwalk Hall started a five-phase, $90 million renovation
project to bring it up to modern concert venue standards. The project
was finished in 2001 (though construction was halted so that the 1999
Miss American Pageant could be held there).

Boardwalk Hall is used today as it was when it first opened. The
events held on the show floor and stage are the same hodgepodge of
shows, festivals, sports events, and competitions.

The place thrives—and rocks, too. I took in a Jimmy Buffett concert
there in summer 2007. Even though the stage was more Caribbean
cool and margaritas, and the sight of thousands of people moving in
unison to "Fins" was startling, Boardwalk Hall still managed to exude
a sense of history.

Ave., Atlantic City 08104. Los Amigos couldn't look more out of place. Nestled against the bargains and bargain hunters of the outlet stores, this 100-year-old bright pink, green, and yellow Mexican restaurant is the one that looks like the tourist. The cuisine is Mexican and Tex-Mex, and all spicy. The main event is the margaritas, which are big and strong enough to drop you if the shopping didn't get to you first. Lunch, dinner. Late night Mon.–Sat. $$.

Luciano Lamberti's Sunset Marina (609-487-6001; sunsetonthebay.com), 9707 Amherst Ave., Margate 08402. Luciano Lamberti's started in 2000 as a simple pasta house on the bay, but it has since become more of a destination for unique Italian dishes. Many of the traditional recipes have been passed down through the Lamberti family. Go with selections from the pizza menu, or indulge in one of the many pasta dishes, which, according to Italian tradition, are big big big. Lunch, dinner. $$.

Manna (609-822-7722; mannaventnor.com), 7309 Ventnor Ave., Ventnor City 08406. It's New American at this exclusive 20-seat restaurant. The items on the menu change per season to whatever's fresh at the time—the dinner specials are listed on their website. Reservations are recommended, even for lunch, and they're an absolute must for dinner. BYOB. Lunch, dinner. Closed Sun. $$$.

Mia (609-441-2345; miaac

.com), Caesars Atlantic City Hotel Casino, 2100 Pacific Ave., Atlantic City 08401. This über-luxe Mediterranean Italian restaurant is set inside soaring towers at Caesars, which gives your fine dining a light, airy effect. Dinner. Closed Sun.–Mon. $$$.

Ozzie's Luncheonette (609-487-0575), 2401 Atlantic Ave., Long Port 08403. Talk about retro charm. This eatery, which has been serving up breakfast and lunch in Longport for more than 50 years, is decked out in midcentury style with black-and-white-checked floors, red leather seating and stools, and pictures of Long Port from years past on the walls. For breakfast, order anything you can imagine in omelet form. Lunch sandwiches are enough to hold you over until dinner—and then some. I like the I HEART LONGPORT mugs that wait at the counter for your morning cup of coffee. Those seats are prized spots in the restaurant, so get there early to grab one, or be prepared to wait. Breakfast, lunch until 3 PM. $.

Sage (609-823-2110; sage ventnor.com), 5206 Atlantic Ave., Ventnor City 08406. This 75-seat restaurant is the latest creation from Lisa Savage, who was based in Ventnor City for 13 years before trying her luck mainland. She brought the best from that venture to Sage, putting items like fried artichoke hearts and seared scallops on the menu. No credit cards. BYOB. Dinner. Closed Mon. in winter. $$.

Firewater

Like beer? Then Firewater at the Tropicana is a must-visit while you're in Atlantic City. They have 50 beers on tap, and 101 types of brews in bottles.

If you can't decide, tell the bartender your favorite beers, and he or she will make a recommendation. Or peruse the "menu," which is a thick book describing their beers. If you're a sports fan, the TVs are usually tuned into the game of the day, or ESPN. A favorite for bachelorette parties. $.

Tomatoe's Restaurant (609-822-7535; tomatoesmargate.com), 9300 Amherst Ave., Margate 08402. The sushi is the main attraction here. Don't let the size fool you—even though Tomatoe's seats 250 people, you'll still need a reservation, especially in-season. The decor is a mashed-up mix, from kitschy wall murals to Oriental accents. Extensive wine list as well. It's very much a see-and-be-seen place—though it morphs into a cozier locals' hangout in the off-season. Dinner, late night. $$$.

The Trinity (609-345-6900; trinitypubac.com), Pier Shops at Caesars, 1 Atlantic Ocean, Atlantic City 08401. The bar at this Irish pub was imported from Ireland, so Trinity is the real deal. It's a surprising cozy and intimate spot at the Pier, which is better known for its flashy and pricey shops and restaurants. The Trinity shifts over to a bar scene late at night. Call ahead for the live music schedule. Lunch, dinner, late night. $$–$$$.

White House Sub Shop (609-345-1564), 2301 Arctic Ave., Atlantic 08401. It's all about the food at this sub shop, which has been in business since 1946. Frank Sinatra was a fan, and I can see why. The sandwiches are huge and stuffed with meat, cheese, and whatever else you like. The White House Sub Special is always a hit. Even though I ordered a half size, I was full past dinner. No credit cards. Lunch. $.

Don't Miss This

Check out these great attractions and activities . . .

Absecon Light House (609-449-1360; abseconlighthouse.org), 31 S. Rhode Island Ave., Atlantic City 08401. If you're looking for a workout with your view, climb the 228 steps to the top of New Jersey's tallest lighthouse (and third tallest in the United States). It was built by General George Mead in 1857 and looks over both Atlantic City and nearby Brigantine. Open 10 AM–5 PM in-season; 11–4 Thu.–Mon., Sept.–June. $.

Absecon Lighthouse
Courtesy of Atlantic City Convention and Visitors Authority

Atlantic City Cruises (609-347-7600; atlanticcitycruises.com), 800 New Hampshire Ave., Atlantic City 08401. Whether you're looking for a dolphin-watching tour, a morning skyline cruise, or a happy hour on a boat, check out Atlantic City Cruises. They don't go out too far into the ocean if seasickness is a concern. Call ahead if the weather's wonky to make sure the boats are going out that day. See the website for cruise dates and times. $$$.

Atlantic City Outlets: The Walk (609-872-7002; acoutlets.com), 1931 Atlantic Ave., Atlantic City 08401. It's hard to miss the Atlantic City Outlets if you're

Lucy the Elephant

(609-823-6473; lucytheelephant.org), 9200 Atlantic Ave., Margate 08402. In 1881 real estate prospector James Vincent de Paul Lafferty Jr. built a 65-foot-high wooden elephant in Margate, hoping that it would attract visitors and potential real estate buyers. He was right then, and still is today. Lucy's been a tourist attraction, a restaurant, even a home, and is now back to an attraction. She invites visitors to take a walk up inside. Make sure you head into the top—her howdah—to get a 360-degree view of Margate. Guided tours available. Open 10 AM–8 PM Mon.–Sat., 10–5 PM Sun., mid-June–Labor Day. Call for off-season hours. $.

Emil R. Salvini, *Tales of the New Jersey Shore* (Guilford, CT: Globe Pequot Press)

Courtesy of Atlantic City Convention and Visitors Authority

Monopoly

If you've ever passed go to collect $200 or built the elusive hotels on Boardwalk and Park Place, you know your Monopoly. But did you know where the names of the streets came from? Atlantic City.

Philadelphian Charles B. Darrow was an unemployed salesman during the Depression. He traveled to Atlantic City's Steel Pier, which was once an entertainment mecca and today an amusement pier but was then a place where men went to find work. When he returned home—still unemployed—he created the game that is now Monopoly, using Atlantic City's geography as part of the real estate buying and selling game.

At first it was rejected by Parker Brothers for having "52 design errors." So Darrow and a friend made 5,000 sets and sold them to a Philadelphia department store. They sold out, and Parker Brothers took another look.

Since 1935, the first year of the Parker Brothers edition, 275 million games have been sold. And although you can now buy Monopoly games themed to your alma matter, town, or favorite movie, the original Atlantic City version is still the classic.

coming into town from the Atlantic City Expressway: You drive right through them. Make sure you stop if you're looking for a good deal from J.Crew, the Gap, Banana Republic, and Nike, among others. The area that the outlets covers keeps expanding, so visit the website for updated stores, locations, and hours.

Edwin B. Forsythe National Wildlife Refuge (609-652-1665; fws.gov/northeast/forsythe), 800 Great Creek Rd., Oceanville 08231. Two wildlife refuges, which were established in 1939 and 1967, came together in the 1980s to form the 43,000-acre Edwin B. Forsythe National Wildlife Refuge. It's located on one of the Atlantic Flyway's most active flight paths, so it attracts birds and birders from around the world. You can drive, walk, hike or run an 8-mile continuous loop through the refuge, or hike one of the shorter trails. If you're running in summer, make sure to bring hydration. There's no shade. The park is open sunrise–sunset; refuge headquarters, 10–3. $.

IMAX Theatre at Tropicana (609-340-4000; tropicana.net), Tropicana, 2831 Boardwalk, Atlantic City 08401. If you're looking for a break from the fun and sun, or something to do on a rainy day—or if you just want to see the latest blockbuster—head to the IMAX Theatre at the Tropicana. They

Spa Life

Looking to relax? Atlantic City has plenty of spa options. Here are a few highlights:

bluemercury (609-347-7778; bluemercury.com), Quarter at the Tropicana, 2801 Pacific Ave., Atlantic City 08401.

The Chelsea (800-548-3030; thechelsea-ac.com), 111 S. Chelsea Ave., Atlantic City 08401.

Crimzen (800-777-8477; trumpmarina.com), Trump Marina Casino Hotel, Huron and Brigantine Blvd., Atlantic City 08401.

Elizabeth Arden Red Door Spa (609-441-5333; reddoorspas.com), Harrah's Atlantic City, 777 Harrah's Blvd., Atlantic City 08401.

Qua (609-343-2400; caesarsac.com/casinos/caesars-atlantic-city/qua), Caesars Atlantic City, 2100 Pacific Ave., Atlantic City 08401.

Spa at Bally's (609-340-4603; harrahs.com), Bally's Atlantic City), 1900 Boardwalk, Atlantic City 08401.

Spa at Trump Plaza (spa: 609-441-6710; salon: 609-441-6035; trumpplaza.com), Trump Plaza Hotel & Casino, Mississippi Ave. at the Boardwalk, Atlantic City 08401.

Spa, The Waterclub at Borgata (800-800-8817; thewaterclub hotel.com/spa), 1 Renaissance Way, Atlantic City 08401.

Spa Toccare (609-317-7555; theborgata.com), Borgata Resort & Spa Hotel Casino, 1 Borgata Way, Atlantic City 08401.

Immersion at the Water Club   Courtesy of Borgata Hotel Casino & Spa

typically screen whatever brand-new big-budget movie is out (and in 3-D if applicable) as well as a documentary built for the huge IMAX screen. Always check the website before going. They usually offer coupons and group discounts, and you can buy tickets online. $$.

Marine Mammal Stranding Center (609-266-0538; marine mammalstrandingcenter.org), 3625 Brigantine Blvd., Brigantine 08203. Injured whales, dolphins, seals, and turtles found in local waters are brought here for rehab. The public viewing hours are limited for the safety of the animals, but you can also check out the attached shop and exhibits on sea life and how the stranding center works. Open 10 AM–4 PM Mon., Tue., Thu., Fri., and Sat., 10–2 Sun. in-season. Closed Wed. Free, though donations are appreciated.

New Jersey Korean War Memorial (state.nj.us/military/korea), Park Place and the Boardwalk, Atlantic City 08402. The Korean War Memorial is a solemn spot along the Atlantic City Boardwalk, and for obvious reasons. The memorial features a 12-foot-tall soldier clutching dog tags, and a mural of men emerging from a wall. It's a revered spot, and worth visiting. Free.

Pier Shops at Caesars (609-345-3100; thepiershopsatcaesars.com), 1 Atlantic Ocean, Atlantic City 08401. If the Walk is your bargain spot, the Pier is where you can blow your winnings at luxury retailers like Tiffany's, Burberry, and Louis Vuitton. It's also home to an Apple store if you can't live without an iPod or iPhone (or want to give your email a quick check for free). Don't be intimidated by the big names—the Pier is home to mall staples like Banana Republic. You'll also find restaurants on its third floor, and The Show—a water show with lights and music—at the east end of

> **Shave and a Haircut**
>
> Gentlemen, you have the room. Or at least you have these rooms at the Barbershop at the Borgata, which is a guys-only spa and salon. The highlight is the straight-razor shave, which includes a pre-shave oil, then hot towel and aftershave treatment. The Barbershop also offers haircuts plus guy-friendly manicures and pedicures. No one said looking good had to make you girlie, especially if you stop here.

Caesars Atlantic City and the Pier Shops at Caesars   Courtesy of Caesars

Absecon Light House   Wikimedia Commons

the building. Mall open 11 AM–9 PM Mon.–Thu., 11–10 Fri., 10–10 Sat., 10–8 Sun. Hours vary for restaurants.

Quarter at the Tropicana (800-843-8767; tropicana.net), 2801 Pacific Ave., Atlantic City 08401. You'll find everything from spy gear to spa products at this indoor shopping area, which is connected to the restaurant complex that has made the Quarter a popular night spot and a top choice of *Casino Player Magazine*. The Quarter has a few national stores, like White House Black Market, but also shops that are as individual as the shoppers, such as Jake's Dog House. Open 10 AM–11 PM Sun.–Thu., till midnight Fri.–Sat.

48 Hours

DAY 1 Start your day with a buffet. They're legendary, and you can get just about whatever you want. Looking traditional? Go to Resorts. Some of the workers have been there since the first day it turned from hotel into casino. Flashy fare? Head to the Borgata Buffet at—you guessed it—the Borgata.

Then hit the beach. It's *the* thing to do down the shore. If it's raining, or if sand's not your thing, work off that breakfast with a walk up the Absecon Lighthouse. The view from the top of the 228 steps is one of the best you'll get in Atlantic City.

Miss America

She might have left town for Las Vegas, but Miss America is still very much a part of Atlantic City.

The beauty pageant started in Atlantic City in 1921, even if that didn't become the name until the following year. It started as a straight beauty pageant, with talent added in 1935. In 1945, Miss America became a scholarship-granting organization, something the group still pushes (and pushes, and pushes) today. The contest first hit the small screen in 1954 and became one of the longest-running live events in television history. Every September, the chosen winner, in her glittering tiara, waved and cried down a runway at Boardwalk Hall.

I'm not what you would call girlie, but I still watched every September. I made fun of the girls and their unnaturally white smiles and the silliness of a beauty pageant still having so much draw. But apparently I wasn't the only one who thought Miss America was falling out of step with the times. In 2006, after being dropped from her longtime broadcast home of ABC, Miss America moved to Las Vegas and was

RIGHT: Miss America gown at the Sheraton Atlantic City.

Courtesy of *Boardwalk Memories, Tales of the Jersey Shore*—Emil R. Salvini (Globe Pequot Press)

televised on Country Music Television in January, not on the traditional September date. CMT dropped the pageant after one year, and it was picked up by the Learning Channel for 2007, adding in a reality-television element and another January show date. She landed back on ABC in 2010, but still in Sin City.

You can still find pieces of Miss America lore in Atlantic City, most lovingly now in the Miss'D America pageant, which takes place in Boardwalk Hall the day after the official competition. It's a pageant for drag queens. I went in 2011. Yes, I might have watched Miss America when I was a kid, but now? This pageant in Atlantic City is the one to watch; it's a must-see if you're in town in January.

Kitty Hiccups is crowned Miss'd America 2011 in Atlantic City's Boardwalk Hall

Courtesy of Greater Atlantic City GLBT Alliance

If you can get down all 228 steps in time, head over to Atlantic City Cruises for a Morning Skyline trip, which in-season typically sets sail at 11 AM.

I don't know if you'll be hungry for lunch just yet, but if you are, a hoagie at the White House Sub Shop is a must-do. Get a half order. Full order is more than enough for two people.

Since you're already off the Boardwalk, how about some shopping? You can't miss the Atlantic City Outlets: The Walk, which includes outlets of J.Crew, Nike, and Coach. Keep walking up South Michigan Avenue until you get back to the Boardwalk by Caesar's, which across the way extends into the Pier Shops at Caesars. I've sometimes found better bargains on the discount racks in those stores than I have at their outlets on the Walk.

Ready for dinner? If you're looking for a romantic meal, head to the Knife & Fork Inn—but only after you have a cocktail at the Dizzy Dolphin, which is a wonderfully ridiculous bar at the Atlantic City Hilton. If you've got the energy for a nightcap and/or dancing, cab yourself over to the Borgata for several nightlife options: live music at the Gypsy Bar, high-energy dance at the Mixx, or lounge-style club life at mur.mur.

If you're bringing the kids along, try dinner at Carmine's at the Tropicana, which serves family-style dinners, then finish up with a flick at the IMAX Theatre, which is also at the Trop.

An aerial view of Atlantic City, including the Steel Pier   Courtesy of Marc Steiner/Agency New Jersey

DAY 2

More food to start day 2? Of course. This is vacation. For bagels and on-the-go fare, try Adam Good Deli at the Trop, which won't gouge you on prices and gets you what you need. Then head down to Margate to visit the grande dame of the Jersey Shore: Lucy, the 65-foot wooden elephant. Don't forget the museum store located at her feet. You don't need to have kids with you to visit. I recommend it to everyone. It's quintessential Jersey Shore.

For lunch stop off at Down Beach Deli, also in Margate. If you like spicy things, you'll love the peppers that come out before your meal. Then it's back to the Boardwalk for a stroll and some people-watching—or you might check out the musicians and performers who set up along the way. Make sure to stop at the New Jersey Korean War Memorial, which is located at where Park Place meets the Boardwalk. If you like rides, head to the Steel Pier, which has dozens and is an important part of Atlantic City history.

Dinner on your last night is at Capriccio for knockout food with a great view. For nightlife, take a walk down the Boardwalk to Dusk, located inside Caesars. Always expect good DJs. Sometimes expect D-list celebrities and their entourages, which can be incredibly entertaining.

The Jitney

What are all those little blue buses zipping around Atlantic City? No, they're not senior services vehicles or errand trucks. They're a cheap, easy, and efficient way to get around town.

The Atlantic City Jitney Association started in 1915, and it's the longest-running nonsubsidized transit company in the country. There's even a Jitney in the Smithsonian Institution.

Today the fleet is made up of 13 state-of-the-art, air-conditioned, 13-passenger vehicles. They run 24 hours a day, 365 days a year, and stop all over Atlantic City, including all the casinos. They are wheelchair accessible and cost $2.25 a ride. That's far from a nickel, which is what the word *jitney* means in Old English, but it's still cheap.

Extend Your Stay

If you have more time, try these great places to see and things to do . . .

Take some time out to relax by hitting Qua, the super-luxurious spa at Caesars. If you only have time for a quick mani-pedi, your best bet is bluemercury at the Tropicana. Guys, you can get in on the relaxation act, too: The Barbershop at the Borgata has a men's-only treatments.

The best bloody Marys on the island by far are at the Chelsea, which has pool parties with DJs during the day on summer weekends. You *must* get there early to get a seat, or pay to reserve a cabana.

Ready to drink on the beach? You can't quite do that legally in Atlantic City, but you can hit the Beach Bar at Trump Plaza, which was voted one of the 21 sexiest bars in the world by the Travel Channel.

Special Events

Festivals, parties, and happenings down the shore

YEARLY

February

Atlantic City Group Wedding (609-348-7100). On February 14 every year, Atlantic City sponsors a group wedding. Yes, it's legal, though you have to make arrangements in advance. Whether you want to get married in jeans and T-shirts or will do the whole tux-and-white-gown deal, they're ready for you.

March

St. Patrick's Day Parade (888-AC-VISIT; saintpatricksdayparade.com/AtlanticCity/index.htm), Atlantic City Boardwalk. Everyone's Irish on St. Patrick's Day. Show your pride at this annual event, which starts at 1 PM on the Boardwalk at New Jersey Avenue and ends at Albany Avenue. Free.

Atlantic City beach in winter

Thunder over the Boardwalk   Courtesy of Marc Steiner/Agency New Jersey

April

Atlantic City Easter Parade (609-347-5300), Atlantic City Boardwalk. Get decked out in your Easter finest, or watch the "Best Dressed" contestants stroll down the Boardwalk at this annual tradition. The parade starts at 2 PM at Indiana Avenue. Free.

July

Chicken Bone Beach Jazz Series (609-441-9064; chickenbonebeach.org), Kennedy Plaza at Missouri Avenue and the Boardwalk, Atlantic City 08401. Until the early 1950s, African Americans were not allowed on all sections of the beach in Atlantic City, so they stayed on the Missouri Avenue area of the beach. It became known as Chicken Bone Beach, a name that sticks even today, and it was recognized as a historic site by the city in 1997. It's the center of weekly jazz concerts on Thursday nights in-season on the Boardwalk. Free.

August

Atlantic City Air Show (609-345-4524; atlanticcityairshow.com), Atlantic City Boardwalk. US Air Force Thunderbirds and US Navy Blue Angels soar and zip over the Atlantic City Boardwalk and coast at this spectacular event. Air show fans will know that having both groups at one show is a rarity—and because of it, this is the largest military flying event in New Jersey. Free.

    Puerto Rican Parade and Latin Music Festival (609-347-0770; atlanticcityparade.com), Atlantic City Boardwalk. Puerto Rican and Latin heritage are celebrated at this two-pronged event. A parade on the Boardwalk starts at noon, followed by a Latin Music Festival. Free.

October

Atlantic City Marathon (609-601-1RUN; atlanticcitymarathon.org). Think you've got what it takes to run 26.1 miles in one shot? Give it a try at this annual marathon. The course sometimes changes, so check out their website to find out where you'll start—and where you'll go. $$$.

Atlantique City Spring Antiques and Collectables Show (800-526-2724), Atlantic City Convention Center. This is the big one—the largest indoor art, antiques, and collectibles show in the world. Twice a year exhibitors come from as far away as Asia to partake in buying and selling items from the 18th, 19th, and 20th centuries. $$.

Oktoberfest (609-748-6160), Historic Towne of Smithville, 615 E. Moss Mill Rd., Smithville 08205. Taste the best of German food and drink in a family-friendly setting at this festival, which also draws about 100 art and craft vendors to Smithville.

Important Info

Where to turn when you need to know

EMERGENCY NUMBERS

In an emergency, dial 911.
Poison information: 800-222-1222
Non-emergency police: 609-347-5780

HOSPITALS

AtlantiCare Regional Medical Center—City Campus (609-345-4000; atlanticare.org), 1925 Pacific Ave., Atlantic City 08401.

NEWSPAPERS

Atlantic City Weekly (609-646-4848; acweekly.com).
Press of Atlantic City (609-272-7000; pressofatlanticcity.com).

TRANSPORTATION

ACES Train (877-326-7428; acestrain.com).
Atlantic City Airport Taxi & Car Service (877-568-8294; actaxi.com).
Atlantic City International Airport (609-645-7895; acairport.com).
Atlantic City Jitney (609-344-8642; jitneys.net).
Avis (609-383-9356; avis.com).

The Haddon-Chalfonte Hotel gave stately background to the beach. It's now Resorts.
Courtesy of Jen A. Miller

Budget (609-383-0682; budget.com).
Enterprise Rent-A-Car (609-348-2902; enterprise.com).
Hertz (609-646-7733; hertz.com).
New Jersey Transit Rail (800-772-2222; njtransit.com).
New Jersey Transit Bus (800-772-2222; njtransit.com).
Philadelphia International Airport (215-937-6937; phl.org).
Tropiano Transportation Airport Shuttle (800-559-2040; tropiano
transportation.com).

TOURISM CONTACTS

Atlantic City Convention and Visitors Authority (888-228-4748; atlantic
citynj.com).
Atlantic City Regional Mainland Chamber of Commerce (609-345-4524;
atlanticcitychamber.com).
Brigantine Beach Tourism Commission (800-847-5198; brigantinebeach
nj.com).
New Jersey Travel and Tourism (800-VISITNJ; state.nj.us/travel).

2

Ocean City

FAMILY FUN

Including Somers Point

HISTORY

OCEAN CITY was founded as a Christian retreat. While the laws set down by the town's four Methodist founders are no longer standing, they have influenced present-day Ocean City. Its 2.5-mile boardwalk doesn't have any of the seedy T-shirt shops and tattoo parlors that are popular in some Jersey Shore towns, and the boardwalk has consistently been ranked one of the best in the country. The entire town was voted Best Family Beach by the Travel Channel, and *Coastal Living* magazine named it as one of its top 31 best beach vacation towns.

The bay in Ocean City
Courtesy of City of Ocean City, NJ

Ocean City is a barrier island, surrounded by the Atlantic Ocean on the east and Great Egg Harbor Bay on the west. This provides ample opportunities to enjoy water sports like wave running, boating, fishing, surfing, and swimming.

The 7.5-mile-long island was first known as Peck's Beach, named after John Peck, who staged his whaling operations here. Since its incorporation in 1897, Ocean City has been a dry town. In early 2011, a band of restaurant owners pressed the BYOB rules and were staunchly shut out by the city council. This doesn't just mean you won't find bars or liquor stores on the island. You are also not allowed to bring alcohol into

LEFT: Ocean City boardwalk

Ocean City Boardwalk   Courtesy of Marc Steiner/Agency New Jersey

restaurants and certainly not to the beach. Even if Ocean City has been described as "the wettest dry town down the shore," this no-liquor rule has helped it remain a for-families spot.

The main attraction, aside from the beach, is the boardwalk. In-season, it's a beautiful jumble of shops, restaurants, amusements, and people. On summer mornings, bikes and surreys zip up and down the boards. At night, the boardwalk is packed with people getting from one spot to another, or just taking in the sights.

You'll be hard-pressed to find über-fine dining in Ocean City (the liquor situation has a lot to do with that), though the town is chock-full of casual, hearty restaurants, and almost all are kid-friendly. Plus, it's 10 miles from Atlantic City, or you can explore one of the eateries (with liquor licenses) in Somers Point, just on the other side of the bay.

Pick Your Spot

Best places to stay in and around Ocean City

Atlantis Inn Luxury Bed & Breakfast (609-399-9871; atlantisinn.com), 601 Atlantic Ave.,

Ocean City 08226. Luxury, luxury, luxury at this expansive and expensive inn. The price tag is worth it if it's elegance you're after. You might not even want to leave your room, since those at Atlantis include Jacuzzi whirlpool tubs for two, fireplaces, and a grand poster or sleigh bed draped in luxury sheets import-

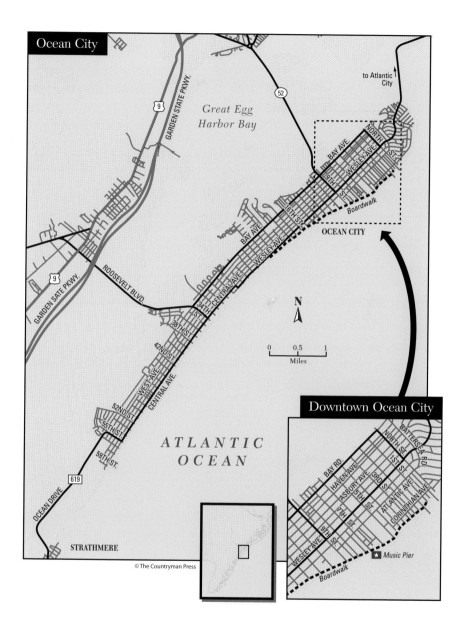

Ocean City

Great Egg
Harbor Bay

to Atlantic
City

GARDEN STATE PKWY.

BAY AVE.
WESLEY AVE.
NORTH ST.
19TH ST.
6TH ST.
Boardwalk

OCEAN CITY

BAY AVE.
WESLEY AVE.
CENTRAL AVE.

ROOSEVELT BLVD.

GARDEN SATE PKWY.

34TH. ST.
38TH ST.
42ND. ST.

N

0   0.5   1
Miles

WEST AVE.
CENTRAL AVE.
52ND ST.
55TH ST.
59TH ST.

OCEAN DRIVE

ATLANTIC
OCEAN

Downtown Ocean City

BATTERSEA RD.
NORTH ST.
1ST ST.
BAY RD.
HAVEN AVE.
ASBURY AVE.
5TH ST.
3RD ST.
ATLANTIC AVE.
CORINTHIAN AVE.

WESLEY AVE.
6TH ST.

★ Music Pier

Boardwalk

STRATHMERE

© The Countryman Press

ed from Milan. Atlantis also has an in-house spa. $$$$.

Bayberry Inn (877-229-6265; bayberryinnoc.com), 811 Wesley Ave., Ocean City 08226. This inn offers two kinds of rooms—classic nautical or romantic Victorian. The

Bayberry, which was built in the early 1900s, is also ideal for a quick trip to Ocean City. While most other accommodations require a two-night stay in-season, you can just drop in for one here, as long as it's a weekday trip. In 2010, they added a weekly rental option for a one-bedroom apartment. Open in-season; weekends only Sept.–mid-Oct. $$–$$$.

Beach Club Hotel (609-399-8555; beachclubhotel.com), 1280 Boardwalk, Ocean City 08226. This hotel is literally on the beach, or as close as you can get to it—the boardwalk is your closest neighbor. The rooms are clean and smoke-free. Nothing too fancy, but with the beach outside, are you really going to spend much time in your room? They also have grown-up and kiddie pools, both with ocean views. Open in-season. $$–$$$$.

Beach Club Suites (609-399-4500; beachclubsuites.com), 1217 Ocean Ave., Ocean City 08226.

Consider this an upgraded version of the rooms at the Beach Club Hotel (both places are owned by the same company). The accommodations are one-room apartments with kitchens, living rooms with pullout sofa, and separate bedroom. You can get connecting apartments, too, if you're with a large group. Like the Beach Club Hotel, it has a pool and ocean views. Open in-season. $$–$$$$.

Flanders Hotel (609-399-1000; theflandershotel.com), 719 E. 11th St., Ocean City 08226. This hotel, which opened in 1923, has survived fire, the stock market crash, and a partial conversion into condominiums to remain as one of the more luxurious places to stay in Ocean City. It retains the opulence and

Ocean City beach   Courtesy of Marc Steiner/Agency New Jersey

Flanders Hotel. Courtesy of James T. Hoffman

glamour that befit Grace Kelly and Jimmy Stewart, who both stayed here. One of the more popular year-round hotels. $$$$.

Osborne's Fairview Inn (609-398-4319; osbornesinn.com), 601 E. 15th St., Ocean City 08226. If you've got kids, check out Osborne's Inn. One of their apartments is stocked with cribs, high chairs, and toys. The Osbornes, who have been running the inn for more than 30 years, keep this apartment ready for visits from their own kids and grandkids; otherwise it's available to rent. As for the other accommodations, you'll find both rooms and apartments for however many guests—of whatever age—you're bringing. Open in-season. Rentals year-round. $$.

Pier 4 on the Bay (888-927-9141; pier4hotel.com), 6 Broadway, Somers Point 08244. Pier 4 is a four-story hotel that first popped up on the bay in Somers Point in 1972. It was recently renovated to bring it up to the standards of today's Jersey Shore visitor. Every room has a balcony; a private pool and sundeck face the bay. $$–$$$.

Scarborough Inn (800-258-1558; scarboroughinn.com), 720 Ocean Ave., Ocean City 08226. This AAA Three Diamond bed & breakfast has been welcoming visitors to Ocean City since 1895. The rooms are well appointed, but not overly fussy in the romance department. There are a few rooms with two beds, too, if your stay will be more platonic. Check out the family photos on the corridor that leads from the living room area to the first-floor rooms and kitchen. Open in-season. $$$.

The Lady in White

Is the Flanders Hotel haunted? According to the staff, yes.

They don't say that like it's a bad thing. The in-hotel restaurant is even named after Emily, aka the Lady in White, their "happy ghost." She has long brown hair and wears a white dress with no shoes; she's been known to go in and out of walls, unscrew lightbulbs, and sing. She's never really caused any trouble, though she allegedly appeared in a wedding picture taken in one of the hotel's banquet halls.

To get a look at her, visit the second floor of the Flanders to see a portrait painted by Tony Troy. Or just hang around the hotel, which is the best way to encounter the young lady.

Local Flavors

Taste of the town—local restaurants, cafés, bars, bistros, etc.

The Anchorage (609-926-1776), 823 Bay Ave., Somers Point 08244. This is the kind of laid-back bar you can visit in- or off-season and still feel at home. It's located across the street from the bay in Somers Point. The pub grub is always good and the beer, forever cold. Great place to watch sporting events, or stay up way past your bedtime. Open 11 AM–2 AM.

Bloom 'n Tulip (609-399-4953), 1001 Ocean Ave., Ocean City 08226. A big part of Bloom 'n Tulip's charms is that it looks like it's been here forever. Coffee still comes in a carafe, and mugs are on the table. I expected someone to come out of the kitchen and call me "hon"—it's that homey. The food is diner staples, like pancakes and BLTs. It's a cool spot near the beach to grab a bite to eat that doesn't involve a paper plate. They do take-out, too. Breakfast, lunch, dinner mid-May–Columbus Day. $.

Brown's (609-391-0677), 110 Boardwalk, Ocean City 08226. The doughnuts are the star attraction at this boardwalk-side eatery. They come hot out of the oven, and each one is dipped into whatever you like, whether it be vanilla, chocolate, cinnamon sugar, or a host of other sweet toppings. Or you could go with plain, but why be boring? They serve lunch, too, but it's the doughnuts that draw the long lines (avoid them by being an early bird). No credit cards. Breakfast, lunch in-season. $.

The Chatterbox (609-399-0113), 500 E. 9th St., Ocean City 08226. It's almost not a vacation in Ocean City without at least one

9th St Bridge, before recent causeway construction. Courtesy of James T. Hoffman

Cape May County Dog Park

(oceancitydogpark.org) 45th St. and Haven Ave., Ocean City 08226. Even though dogs aren't allowed on most beaches at the South Jersey Shore in-season, Ocean City has a spot for your four-legged friends to play. At the Cape May County Dog Park, you can let your dog off-leash to run, sniff, play, and do tricks on ramps and hurdles. The park has three play areas: one for large dogs, one for small pups, and a dog run for everyone.

To gain access to the park, you must apply for a "Paw Pass" at City Hall (609-399-6112), 861 Asbury Ave., Ocean City 08226. Bring a municipal dog license, which can be from your own municipality, and proof of up-to-date immunizations.

meal at the Chatterbox. It's hard to miss. The building is big, bright, and pink. The food is classic American surf-and-turf with a lot of good sandwiches, a knockout burger, and breakfast items. Breakfast, lunch, dinner. Closed Mondays off-season. $.

Dot's Pastry Shop (609-399-0770), 3148 Asbury Ave., Ocean City 08226. It's worth waiting at this take-a-number bakery for their rich desserts, cookies, and cakes. Cash only. Open 7 AM–5 PM Mon.–Sat. and 7–2 Sun. in-season. Weekends only off-season. $.

Corson's Inlet State Park

(609-861-2404; state.nj.us/dep/parksandforests/parks/corsons.html), Ocean City and Upper Township, Cape May County. Corson's Inlet is 341 acres of undeveloped oceanfront land. It was preserved in 1969. Good thing, as most of the South Jersey Shore is now developed to the max. Corson's is home to sand dune systems, marine estuaries, and upland areas, including all the critters that live therein. It's a great spot for birding, especially in spring and fall. You'll also find a boat ramp, hiking trails, tours, saltwater fishing and crabbing spots, and catamaran boat storage areas.

Johnson's Popcorn (800-842-2676; johnsonspopcorn.com), 1368 Boardwalk, Ocean City 08226. This isn't exactly movie theater popcorn. Instead of salt, the kernels are doused in hot caramel. It's a treat that's been delighting shore visitors for more than 40 years. Their flagship store is on the Ocean City boardwalk (and open year-round), though you can buy it in other establishments throughout the shore region, and online. They have flavors other than caramel—peanut crunch, chocolate drizzle, and cheddar—but if you're only going for one, go for the classic. Open 10 AM until the crowds go away in-season, 10 AM–4 PM off-season. $.

Kessel's Korner (609-398-1170; kesselskorner.com), 2760 Asbury Ave., Ocean City 08226. Sit at a leather booth with red-and-white-checked tablecloths, or eat in at the small counter. Either way, Kessel's is always packed. They offer take-out for desserts, too, like impossibly thick milk shakes and Breyers ice cream. No credit cards. Open 8 AM until the last customer is served. $.

Kohr Bros. (kohrbros.com), five locations along the Ocean City boardwalk. Kohr started in 1917 in York, Pennsylvania, when Archie Kohr bought an ice cream machine and included the homemade dessert with his family's milk delivery services. Archie and his brother Elton made some adjustments to the recipe, and the machine, and came up with a soft-serve product. The addition of eggs stiffened the ice cream (that's why it's called frozen custard), which helps it stand up in that swirl. It's also lower in sugar and fat than regular ice cream. For the best of both worlds, try the vanilla chocolate swirl. Hours vary. Open in-season. $.

Mack & Mancos (609-399-2548; mackandmancos.com), 758, 920, and 12th & the Boardwalk, Ocean City 08226. The most famous pizza pie on the Ocean City

A slice at Mack & Mancos

concept of crêpes on its head—it's not just a breakfast meal anymore. Try the seafood variety for dinner. It's an interesting mix. Breakfast, lunch, dinner in-season. Call for off-season hours. $.

Ocean City Coffee (609-399-5533; oceancitycoffee.com), 928 Boardwalk, Ocean City 08226. With wooden walls decorated with burlap coffee bean bags, and a roaster on the showroom floor, Ocean City Coffee feels more like a coffeehouse than a boardwalk stop. Open 6 AM–11 PM in-season. Call for off-season hours. $.

Positively Fourth Street Café (609-399-8400; web.mac.com/laurelbay400/cafe-home.html), 400 Atlantic Ave., Ocean City 08226. Yes, *positively* is part of the name of this corner café. Breakfast is big here—thick-cut oatmeal, egg sand-wiches, and of course lots caffeinated drinks are on the menu. They also dish up lunch and, in-season, din-ner. Even if you drink your coffee black, check out the area with the cream and sugar—set up on a bro-ken surfboard held up by man-nequin legs. Open Mon.–Sat. 6:30 AM–9 PM, Sun. till 1 PM.

Red's Jersey Mex (609-399-2272; rojosjerseymex.com), 11th St. and Haven Ave., Ocean City 08226. Sound like an odd mash-up? Who cares about the name—it works. Get tacos, breakfast burritos, que-sadillas, and more at this spot, which is open year-round. No cred-it cards. Open 10 AM–10 PM in-season, 11–9 off-season. $–$$.

boardwalk came here in 1956 when Anthony Mack and Vincent Manco brought their tomato pie from Trenton to the shore. Don't worry if you've got sandy feet—Mack & Mancos is built for the beachgoer. Watching the pizzas being made, with sauce put on top of the cheese via a sauce hose, is half the fun. Lunch, dinner, late night in-season. The 12th Street location is open year-round. $.

Ma France Creperie (609-399-9955), 506 9th Ave., Ocean City 08226. This restaurant turns the

Sindia Courtesy of Emil R. Salvini, *Tales of the New Jersey Shore* (Guilford, CT: Globe Pequot Press)

Sindia Restaurant (609-399-1997; sindiarestaurant.com), 801 Plymouth Pl., Ocean City 08226. You'll find classic American cuisine and a lot of seafood at this longtime Ocean City eatery. Not a meat or seafood lover? Try the pastas, which will keep you full until the next day. Breakfast, dinner, May–Oct. $$.

Smitty's Clam Bar (609-927-8783), 910 Bay Ave., Somers Point 08244. Sure, you could eat inside the dining room, but the best spot is at the outdoor counter where you can watch your seafood being prepared. Their specialty, of course, is the clams. Eat them raw, steamed, fried, or as part of clam chowder or clam burgers. If you're

looking for a bite before heading out on the water, the Breakfast Shop is located at the back of the building, overlooking the water. No credit cards. Breakfast, lunch, dinner in-season. $.

Voltaco's (609-399-0743; voltacositalianfoods.com), 957 West Ave., Ocean City 08226. You'll find unforgettable Italian take-out at this small box of a shop. The sandwiches rule at lunchtime, but it's the specials that will bring a bit of the Old Country to your dinner table: baked spinach ravioli, stuffed shells, manicotti, baked ziti—it's pure Italian goodness. No credit cards. Open 9 AM–8 PM in-season, weekends in fall. $.

Don't Miss This

Check out these great
attractions and activities . . .

Air Circus (609-399-9343), 1114 Boardwalk, Ocean City 08226. If you see kites flying near the board- walk, you're probably watching the best of Air Circus's wares on dis- play. This boardwalk store has been selling kites of all stripes, from your basic high-in-the-sky kite to stunt models, since 1977. They also stock any- thing you could need to make your beach time more creative, like Frisbees and juggling toys. Open 9 AM–11:30 PM in-season. Call for off-season hours.

B&B Department Store (609-391-0046), 827 Asbury Ave., Ocean City 08226. You'll find clothes for the entire family at this large but packed store. Make sure you look up. You won't be able to help it with the critters and modes of transportation hanging from the ceiling. Open 9 AM–10 PM in-season. Call for off-season hours.

Bayside Center (609-525-9244; oceancitychamber.com/baysidecenter .asp), 520 Bay Ave., Ocean City 08226. This 1.35-acre area is both a history and an ecology lesson. The Bayside Center includes the Bay Window Envi- ronment Center, which is a museum that also runs summer camps for kids. They also have a butterfly garden where you can eat lunch on one of the many picnic tables. The grounds are a popular spot to watch the annual

Courtesy of James T. Hoffman

The *Sindia*

The *Sindia* was a 329-foot, four-masted ship that hit a sandbar and cracked in two in Ocean City during a storm in 1901. You can't see the ship from shore anymore—it's been covered by sand—but its remains are around the 16th and 17th Street area. The Sindia restaurant is named after the ship.

Ocean City Music Pier

The Ocean City Music Pier is a one-stop spot in Ocean City. The building, which is located at 9th Street on the Boardwalk, provides shade and benches for weary travelers, and to those looking to take in the view. It also has public bathrooms, a show space for concerts, fairs, and festivals, and an information center that is chock-full of information for your Ocean City vacation. I recommend picking up one of the coupon books. You'll find everything from free rides to restaurant discounts.

Music Pier   Courtesy of Chris Barrett

Night in Venice parade, which is held each July, and for kayakers looking to paddle up for a break. Open 10 AM–4 PM from the last Saturday in June through Labor Day.

Bernie's Barber Shop (609-399-7032), 937 Asbury Ave., Ocean City 08226. Step back in time at this old-fashioned barbershop—yes, with the old chairs and spinning barber pole outside the shop. Open 8 AM–4:30 PM Mon.–Fri.; Sat. by appointment only.

Boardwalk Peanut Shoppe (609-391-2002; boardwalkpeanuts.com), 986 Boardwalk, Ocean City 08226. Those roasters aren't just for show. The 100-plus-year-old machines, which were originally used for coffee, still roast peanuts—in the shell—as they have since the 1930s when they were in the original Atlantic City Boardwalk Planters Peanut Store. You can pick up the freshly roasted peanuts, or chocolate-covered strawberries and bananas. Open 9:30 AM–11:30 PM in-season. $.

Bookateria Too (609-398-0121), 1052 Asbury Ave., Ocean City 08226. Get a deal on your beach reads at this bookstore, which has both new and used titles. All new books are 15 percent off. Used paperbacks are half price, or $1.87 with sufficient trade. Open 9 AM–8 PM Mon.–Fri., 9–6 Sat.

Asbury Avenue

Asbury Avenue is a main street throwback. It's what it a lot of American downtowns looked like when there were no indoor malls, strip malls, four-lane highways through the middle of town, or online shopping.

Its location near the shore and relatively far from any mall has probably helped preserve its main street status, even if blue laws kept the shops closed on Sundays until the 1980s.

What will you find? Just about everything, including kids' clothes, ladies' fashions, antiques, an independent new- and used-book store, and a lot of places to eat. The stores are open year-round, too, unlike most places on the boardwalk, and make for great strolling on a spring or fall day, as well as in summer.

Asbury Avenue   Courtesy of City of Ocean City, NJ

Running at the Shore

I'm a runner. Lucky for me, the shore is a haven for those of us who want to get out and pound asphalt under the heat of the summer sun.

But the conditions down the shore are unlike what you'll face at home. The weather, the tourists, the wind, and the sand all present obstacles. Here are a few tips on how to train by the sea:

• **Beware the sand.** Sure, running on the beach might sound like a romantic idea in that "I'll be able to clear my mind," *Chariots of Fire* kind of way. But it can be hard on your calves and knees, especially if you choose to run on the hard-packed sand by the water's edge—it's on a slope. If you are going to give beach running a go, make sure you mix in some boardwalk or street time; your legs will thank you. If you're a huge fan of beach running, you might want to try the Captain Bill Gallagher Island Run, which takes place in Sea Isle City every August. Seven miles of the 10-mile course are on the beach. It can be a killer, though, especially if it's held on a hot and humid day. I learned that one the hard way.

The author at the end of the Ocean Drive 10 Miler. Courtesy of Mary Miller

• **Beware the tourists.** Whether they're driving, walking, or biking, you need to be aware of the people around you because the streets are packed in season, and the last thing you want to do is get hit. Be especially careful in Ocean City if you're running in the streets because the combination of heavy traffic, narrow streets, and parked cars blocking views around corners can be dangerous. Do whatever you can to stay out of the bike lanes in Avalon—I've almost been run over by a few bikers.

• **Check the wind.** They don't call them "ocean breezes" for nothing—and a headwind during your run can push you along or hold you back. If you're going to run by the water, make sure that you run the route in both directions so you'll be fighting the wind one way only. I tried going up Dune Drive and down Ocean Drive in Avalon for one run. I had the ocean wind in my face on Dune Drive, but I didn't get the same push back on Ocean Drive because it didn't get the sea breezes. Misery.

• **Heat trap.** Even if shore towns are close to the water, they are still prone to heat and humidity. Stay tuned to the weather forecast, and make sure to check for the possibility of afternoon thunderstorms. If you're spending a lot of time in the sun, or in the bars, you might want to recalculate your hydration. Both sun and fun can take a lot out of you, which could dehydrate you before a run.

• **Boardwalk bounce.** I write about health and fitness and was told by one sports doctor that the absolute best place to run is on wooden boardwalks. Why? Because the wood gives, and since the boards are suspended in air, the combined effect is much more cushioning than running on asphalt, concrete, or sand. Atlantic City, Ocean City, and Wildwood have the most distance to offer runners on their board-walks, but be careful of *when* you run, especially if you're going in-season. Mornings belong to bikes and surreys, and nighttime brings crowds that can be difficult to navigate through when walking, let alone running. I've found that bright and early—like before 6 AM—is best in-season.

• **Map your routes online.** You don't need to use your car's odometer to measure how far you'll go. Go to www.gmap-pedometer.com and punch in the name of your shore town. It's easier to see a bird's-eye view of where you're visiting and where you'll be running. I usually run with a Garmin 405 Forerunner. It's a GPS watch that tracks how far you go, and how fast.

• **Run the course.** The spring, summer, and fall bring plenty of races—both running and triathlon—to the shore, so check with towns' chambers of commerce to see what kinds of 5ks, fun runs and dis-tance runs they have scheduled for the summer. The Ocean Drive Marathon, in March, is a great way to cap off a fall/winter/spring train-ing season and to kick off the summer. And what better way to take in the sights than by foot?

Check out njshorerun.com for a complete list of shore races.

Gillian's Island Water Park   Courtesy of Ocean City, NJ

The Ferris wheel at Gillian's Wonderland Pier   Courtesy of City of Ocean City, NJ

Gillian's Island Water Park (609-399-0483; gillianswaterpark.com), 728 Boardwalk, Ocean City 08226. Sometimes it's too hot for the ocean, or the kids think the waves are too small for a real adventure. That's where Gillian's Island Water Park comes in. It has four different water rides for slipping and sliding, plus a kids' area and lazy river if your idea of relaxing is floating the day away while the slides tire the younger ones out. Gillian's also offers private cabanas to rent, each one including lounge chairs, lockers, and ceiling fans. Open in-season, staring in June. Call for hours. $$.

Gillian's Wonderland Pier (609-399-7082; gillians.com), 600 Boardwalk, Ocean City 08226. A longtime favorite with thrills for the entire family. They have plenty of rides for the little kids that won't put you to sleep, either, like Little Wheel, Wonders Lil' Express, Wacky Worm Roller Coaster, and, of course, the classic Carousel, which has been delighting families since 1926. If your older kids need a jolt, there's still the Runaway Train Coaster, Sling Shot, and Canyon River Falls. Open Palm Sunday–mid-Oct. Call for in-season hours—they vary depending on day of the week and month. $.

Jilly's Arcade (609-399-2814; jillysarcade.com), 1168 Boardwalk, Ocean City 08226. You'll find video game piers all over the South Jersey Shore boardwalks, but Jilly's is a classic. It's been keeping kids (and adults) entertained since 1976. It has the latest and greatest must-play games, some less techie games like skee-ball and air hockey, and, in the back room, classics like Ms. Pac-Man, Asteroid, X-Men, the Simpsons, and pinball. Open 24

The Carousel

For most amusement parks, it's all about providing the latest and greatest thrill. How high can we fling you in the air? How fast can we push you? How far do you want to drop?

This is certainly the case on the Ocean City boardwalk. But Gillian's Wonderland Pier still keeps an important piece of history secure on its grounds, one that offers a more sedate ride experience in a classic setting: the carousel.

The carousel was built in 1926 by the Philadelphia Toboggan Company. Today Philadelphia Toboggan Coasters makes death-defying thrill rides you'll find around the country. But from 1904 to 1934, they made 87 wooden carousels, 32 of which are still in operation. Wonderland Pier has number 75.

The carousel first spun in Dallas, Pennsylvania, where it stayed until a move to Rolling Green Park in Selinsgrove in 1946. It came to Ocean City in 1972.

If you're on one of the outer horses, you can still try to reach out and catch the rings. It's one of the last carousels in the country that has a "ring arm," which feeds rings for riders to grab. Grab the brass one and you win free ride tickets. You must be strapped in or you risk falling out into the crowd.

The carousel has been beautifully maintained, and you can hear its calliope music from the boardwalk. No matter what age you are, it's worth its weight in tickets.

hours in-season. Call for off-season hours. Check their website for a free video game coupon. $.

Ocean City Historical Museum (609-399-1801; ocnjmuseum.org), 1735 Simpson Ave., Ocean City 08226. Learn about Ocean City's past at this museum, which features two permanent exhibits. Sea View and Salt Air: A History of Ocean City combines the town's time line with artifacts, photographs, and storyboards to show and tell the town's history. The second exhibit is about the *Sindia*, a four-masted barque that grounded itself in Ocean City in 1901. The museum features temporary rotating exhibits, too. Open 10 AM–4 PM Tue.–Fri., 11–2 Sat. Free.

Only Yesterday (609-398-2869), 1108 Boardwalk, Ocean City 08226. Step back in time at this antiques store. Their stock includes kitsch like Campbell's Soup bowls and 1950s-era CorningWare, vintage clothes, and magazines. Of course you read them for the articles: Only Yesterday has

Playboy magazines from the 1960s through 2000. They also have a store location at 1137 Asbury Avenue that's open Thu.–Sat. Open 11 AM–11 PM in-season, 11–5 weekends off-season.

Playland's Castaway Cove (609-399-4751; boardwalkfun.com), 936 Boardwalk, Ocean City 08226. This pirate-themed pier has 30 rides for kids, grown-ups, and everyone in between. Looking for big thrills? Try the Double Shot, Gravitron, Hurricane, or Python. They also have go-carts and mini golf for a well-rounded adventure. Open Apr.–early Oct. Call for in-season hours—they vary depending on day of the week and month.

Sea Oats (609-398-8399), 710 Asbury Ave., Ocean City 08226. For more than 25 years, Sea Oats has been supplying clothes, costumes, shoes, and toys for girls and boys. You can't beat the cute factor here, even if you don't have kids. Open 10 AM–8 PM Mon.–Fri., 10–5:30 Sat., and 10–5 Sun. in-season. Open 10 AM–5:30 PM off-season.

Separately Swimwear (609-398-2922), 818 Moorlyn Terrace, Ocean City 08226. This bathing suit shop has a wall of bikinis. You buy by mixing and matching tops and bottoms, depending on what styles you want and what fit (great for those of us whose tops and bottoms don't exactly match the way swimwear makers would like). Open 8:30 AM–11:30 PM in-season.

Shriver's (877-668-2339; shrivers.com), Boardwalk at 9th St., Ocean City 08226. Saltwater taffy and fudge have been sold here since 1898, which makes Shriver's the oldest business on the Ocean City boardwalk. The best part (aside from the candy, of course) is that you can watch the taffy being made in the store. The raw materials are mixed then pulled into long rows of taffy at a rate of 300 to 400 pieces an hour, to be cut, wrapped,

Princess Grace

Ocean City has long been a summertime vacation spot for wealthy and/or well-known Philadelphians. Former Philadelphia mayor and Pennsylvania governor Ed Rendell has a house in Ocean City, as does guru Pat Croce. Literary giants Gay and Nan Talese have a summer residence in town (Gay was born in Ocean City).

But no resident shone as bright or drew as much attention as Grace Kelly, who grew up in Philadelphia and spent her summers in her family's home at the corner of 26th and Wesley. The Hitchcock muse and Oscar winner, who died tragically in a car accident, continued to visit her family once a year, even after she left Hollywood to marry Prince Albert of Monaco.

Saltwater Taffy

Poking saltwater taffy is hard work.

After five minutes of punching holes into what looked like a soft, oversized Louisville Slugger with an ice pick, my triceps ached and sweat wet the lining of my Shriver's baseball hat.

"No, like this," said Igor Dukov, the production manager at Shriver's. He drove in the pick in one motion, punching a deep hole as the machine gently rolled and rocked the taffy, elongating a thick log into a long string ready to be cut and double-wrapped in waxed paper. My efforts left dimples on the taffy's surface. I never quite got the hang of it, even after trying to poke the air out of two 50-pound batches.

My arms might have hurt, and I might not have been the perfect air puncher (Dukov came over every five minutes or so to punch more holes so I wouldn't ruin the batch), but I was living a dream: making saltwater taffy at Shriver's in Ocean City.

Every summer my family made a few trips to Ocean City. Sometime after rides at Wonderland Pier and cones of custard at Kohr Bros., we'd stop at Shriver's to watch the taffy being made. I'd press my fingers and nose up to the window separating the store from the taffy-making room and marvel as the candy was pulled, cut, and wrapped. It's a fast process. The machines cut and

Taffy being made at Shriver's
Courtesy of Marc Steiner/Agency New Jersey

wrap 300 to 400 pieces a minute. In summer Shriver's makes 2,000 pounds of taffy a day.

I always begged my parents for a box, and after shuttling four kids up and down the boardwalk, they were tired enough to oblige. But I was never as enamored of the stuff when I ate it off the boardwalk.

Taffy is sweet, cloying even after the first few pieces, and old saltwater taffy—usually found at the back of the cabinet on Labor Day weekend as we packed up our camper—threatens to pull out fillings. But I made such a big deal about wanting taffy that my mom would force me to eat a few pieces before throwing out the box.

"Never again," I'd swear. Until the next summer, when I'd press my fingers and nose up to the glass and watch the taffy fly by.

I stayed away from saltwater taffy after my parents sold their shore place, but I was hooked after I wrote the first edition of this book. How could I not include Shriver's, or James' or Fralinger's? Even if *I* shied away from saltwater taffy, people still bought tons of it. Just about every candy and taffy store, and a lot of gift shops, hawked boxes of the sticky stuff. So I asked Shriver's if I could join them on the production line—in the name of journalism, of course, not in the name of my five-year-old self—to see what the fuss was all about.

I got my wish. Sort of. The machines are old—most from the 1950s and 1960s—and have their own "personalities" (much like the seat belts in my Honda that only I can get to work), and there wasn't enough time in one day to teach me everything.

Instead I tagged along with Dukov and watched the process. There is no salt water in saltwater taffy. There is no salt, either. The name comes from an 1890s taffy stand on the Atlantic City boardwalk. As tends to happen to spots along the ocean, this one flooded. The next day, as the owner cleaned up, a little girl stopped by and asked for some taffy, which he told her—bitterly, I'm sure—was saltwater taffy. The name stuck.

There might not be salt, but there is plenty of syrup, sugar, and hard fat flakes that Dukov hand-measured and scooped into a boiler that cooks the taffy with steam. The batter comes out as a liquid and is poured into red plastic bins to set until it looks like Vaseline. The taffy hardens as it cools until it can be pulled out of the tub in a solid mass. It's cooled again on tables that have cold water running beneath.

Then the taffy is put on the first puller, which winds it around two rotating arms. This adds air to make it chewy and also allows any flavors or coloring to be mixed in. The taffy is cooled again, preparing it to be put on the final machine, where it is dusted with cornstarch and rolled into the right size for cutting and wrapping. That's where I stood—at the final machine—punching air back out of the taffy so it could be worked through the machine to be cut and wrapped into finger-long pieces without breaking.

continued next page

continued from previous page

There was no veil of secrecy about the process—no signing of a confidentiality agreement or swearing on my firstborn child that I would not share the recipe. There isn't a special sauce. Even if new flavors have been added, the recipe hasn't changed much since 1898, though instead of machines, the taffy used to be pulled by hooks and manpower and was cut and wrapped by hand.

Being that it was spring and a weekday, I wasn't exactly playing to a crowd—just a few adults and two toddlers being pulled in a wagon by their mother. They were transfixed, just as I had been. I even waved, and they smiled back.

Maybe that's where this love comes from: Saltwater taffy *is* the Jersey Shore. Saltwater taffy is tradition. It's being a kid and watching taffy being made. Taffy is so much more than simply candy. It evokes memories of riding the waves on my boogie board, making dinners over a campfire and eating them at picnic tables, my hair still wet from showering in the cramped bathroom of our cramped camper, and nights when I stayed up way past my bedtime on the Ocean City boardwalk to ride the carousel, the Tilt-A-Whirl, or the Flying Bob, and to watch saltwater taffy being made and beg for a box before going to bed still feeling like I was rocking on the waves. That's what saltwater taffy means, all wrapped up in one chewy bite.

It's also about eating it fresh. I ate a piece of chocolate taffy right out of the machine. It pulled instead of stuck, and it was a little gooey so the chocolate flavor rolled around my mouth. It wasn't hard. It didn't suck out my fillings. It was sweet.

I took a box of taffy home, along with chocolate-covered pretzels and sugared rainbow fruit slices. It was too cold to leave the windows down, but I cracked them open just an inch and pretended it was the summer wind blowing through my hair as I ate a few more pieces. I put the rest of the box in my freezer, which is where it will stay until I'm ready to thaw it out and share it with family and friends so they, too, can smell, taste, feel, and remember a bite of summer.

and boxed. If you're not ready to commit to an entire box of saltwater taffy, or if you'd like peanut butter better than licorice, check out the taffy bins by the back of the store. You can make your own box. Open 9 AM–10 PM in-season. Call for off-season hours.

Sun Rose Words & Music (609-399-9190; sunrosebooks.com), 756

Sun Rose Words & Music

Asbury Ave., Ocean City 08226. This is the kind of bookstore that makes you hate the big-box chain stores. It's independent and tailored to the needs of both Ocean City residents and tourists. Of course they have all the latest best sellers, plus classics and good beach reads. Sun Rose also stocks an impressive selection of local titles and is a hub of author readings and signings—all books about the shore area. They sell office supplies, music, cards, and drawing pads and pencils. The kids' section is a delight, no matter how old you are. Open 9 AM–6 PM Mon., Tue., Thu., Sat., Sun.; Wed. 9–8, and Fri. 9–9.

Surf Mall (609-398-1533), 1154 Boardwalk, Ocean City 08226. Whatever is hot this summer, whether it's Crocs, faux faded sweatshirts, or hair wrapping, is at the Surf Mall. It's not an actual mall, but a gutted movie theater wherein different vendors set up shop. The old standbys are the collectibles vendor, who leans heavily on movie and action figure memorabilia; and the music store, whose posters line the back wall and parts of the ceiling of the Surf Mall. The products cover all genres, though they lean heavily, of course, on Jersey boy Bruce "the Boss" Springsteen. Open 9 AM–midnight in-season.

Surf Mall

Surfers Supplies

(609-399-8399; surferssupplies.com) 3101 Asbury Ave., Ocean City 08226. It's not often that you walk into a surf shop and see surf-boards. Well, at least not right away. "In most places, they're in the back. They're the core of our business, so we put them right up front," says Greg Beck, co-owner of Surfers Supplies, a surf shop that has been in business since 1962. Beck and two partners bought the store—it's located in a building more than a century old—from its original owner in 2004, and kept the vibe much the same.

You can rent or buy a board here. They also repair and customize your ride. They stock an impressive selection of wet suits, board shorts, and what Beck calls "après surf," meaning clothes with the surfer in mind—like flip-flops, tanks, tees, and button-up shirts with a cool, casual feel.

If you want a lesson, they'll recommend three top guys to teach you how to hang ten. Beck, who's been working at the store since he graduated from high school, says the best waves are at Waverly Beach on the north end of Ocean City, but that the water can be packed during tourist season. His solution? Get a thicker wet suit and surf in the off-season. "If I didn't have to visit my family in Delaware, I'd be surfing on Thanksgiving and Christmas," he says.

Open 9 AM–8 PM Mon.–Sat., 10–6 Sun.

48 Hours

DAY
1

Start your morning by grabbing a table at Kessel's Korner for a hearty breakfast to carry you through the day. Then, if the main Ocean City beach isn't on your schedule, take a trip down to Corson's Inlet State Park, which is a pre-served beach area that has places to boat, swim, and hike.

Worked up an appetite again yet? Good. Stop by the Chatterbox—a must-do if you're in the Ocean City area. You can't miss the building. It's bright pink. Then take a stroll down Asbury Avenue, which has that quaint downtown feel. If you're looking for a good read, make sure to visit Sun Rose Words & Music while you're on Asbury. Also, stop by B&B Department Store and look up. You won't be disappointed with the fun characters on the ceiling.

Start out your evening on the boardwalk at Jilly's Arcade, where you can play the latest and greatest video games, skee-ball, and classics like

Ocean City boardwalk   Courtesy of Emil R. Salvini, *Tales of the New Jersey Shore* (Guilford, CT: Globe Pequot Press)

Pac-Man 24 hours a day in-season. Then check out the Surf Mall for the latest in whatever's hot with the trendy kids. Stop in at the Ocean City Music Pier to pick up a coupon book in the tourism office.

Then cross to the other side of the boardwalk for a stop at Shriver's. You must pick up some saltwater taffy as a souvenir. Make sure to head to the back of the store so you can watch it being made, too.

Let's keep dinner simple tonight. Walk up to the window of Mack & Mancos for a slice. While waiting, take note of how the pizza is made. It's called Trenton-style—the pizza sauce goes on top of the cheese, and is delivered via a sauce hose.

If you've had enough time to digest, hit Playland's Castaway Cove or Gillian's Wonderland Pier for rides, rides, and more rides. If you've got tweens and teens in your group, Playland might be more their speed. They have stomach-flipping rides like the Double Shot. Gillian's leans more toward kid-friendly rides. No matter which you chose, make sure to end your night on the carousel at Gillian's. It's historic, and one of the few wooden carousels where you can still reach out to grab the golden ring.

You have a few options for a post-ride snack. Top two: a bucket of caramel popcorn from Johnson's, and custard from Kohr Bros.

DAY 2

Start day 2 with a doughnut from Brown's. Yes, you will probably have to wait in line, but it's worth it. Or if you're really into coffee, hit up Positively Fourth Street Café or Ocean

City Coffee, depending on where you are. Both serve up quality brews.

Then head to Gillian's Island Waterpark for a day of slipping and sliding or, if you're looking to catch a break, lazing around in the lazy river. If you'd prefer to get out in the ocean, give Surfer Supplies a call and ask the name of a surfing instructor (or stop in the store—they're the best around).

Lunch today is at Voltaco's. You cannot beat the sandwiches here, and they're perfect after a long day sliding or surfing. Afterward, make a trip out to the Bayside Center, which is part museum and part school focusing on the ecosystems around Ocean City.

After last night, you'll want to keep it low-key, so head over the bridge to the Anchorage in Somers Point. Relax with good food, cold beer, and a lot of sports games on TV.

Extend Your Stay

If you have more time, try these great places to see and things to do . . .

Rent a bike or bring your own to ride up and down the boardwalk. Beware—it's only allowed in the morning, and stick to your lane. They're marked for bikes, surreys, runners and pedestrians.

If you're into the spooky, make a trip to the Flanders Hotel and ask about Emily, the resident ghost. Stick around for lunch, too, in the restaurant named after her.

The Rock Jetty and Fishing Pier at 59th Street Courtesy of James T. Hoffman

Special Events

Festivals, parties, and
happenings down the shore

WEEKLY (IN-SEASON)

Tuesday

Funtastic Tuesdays (609-525-9300; ocnj.us), downtown Asbury Ave. The boardwalk doesn't have all the action in Ocean City. Check out downtown at weekly market days, held on Asbury Avenue with entertainment, face painters, and balloon sculptors. 10 AM–1 PM. Free.

Ocean City Beachwalk (609-525-9300), 59th St. & Central Ave., and the Ocean City and Longport Bridge Parking Lot. Get a guided tour of what lives along the ocean's edge at this twice-weekly tour, which starts in two different locations. The tour is an hour long and run by volunteers. $.

Wednesday

Evenings Along Asbury (609-525-9300; ocnj.us), downtown Asbury Ave. Add a little music to your summer nights at this weekly concert series, which starts mid-July and runs through August. 5–8 PM. Free.

Ocean City Beachwalk (609-525-9300), 59th St. & Central Ave., and the Ocean City and Longport Bridge Parking Lot. Get a guided tour of what lives along the ocean's edge at this twice-weekly tour, which starts in two different locations. The tour is an hour long and run by volunteers. 9 AM. $.

Thursday

Inn-to-Inn and Historic Tour (609-399-2639), 7th St. and Central Ave. Check out the historic sights and inns of Ocean City on this weekly trolley tour. Early July to late August. $$.

Market Days (609-525-9300; ocnj.us), downtown Asbury Ave. The boardwalk doesn't have all the action in Ocean City. Check out downtown at weekly market days, held on Asbury Avenue with entertainment, face painters, and balloon sculptors. 10 AM–1 PM. Free.

YEARLY

January

First Day at the Beach (609-525-9300), Ocean City boardwalk. Just because it's cold doesn't mean the beach is closed. Some people take this literally at the annual first dip. Don't worry—no one will cry foul if you just watch. Free.

March

Jazz at the Point (609-927-7161; somersptschools.org/jazz). This three-day event spreads jazz throughout Somers Point with performances from local and national artists. The festival also sponsors student workshops, and proceeds go to Foundation for Education, a nonprofit organization dedicated to improving local schools. $$.

April

Doo Dah Parade (609-399-1412), Ocean City boardwalk. Death and taxes might be two things you can't avoid in life, but you can kiss tax season good-bye at this annual funny parade, which features more than 500 basset hounds and comic acts parading down Asbury Avenue and the boardwalk. Free.

In Your Easter Bonnet

Easter might be a reason for some people to go to church, but for others it is *the* time to hit the Ocean City boardwalk. Almost every store and restaurant is open, catering to crowds looking for an early dose of spring, or lining up to buy discounted tickets to Playland's Castaway Cove or Gillian's Wonderland Pier.

Somers Point Bayfest (888-300-9010; somerspointbayfest.org), Bay Ave. Eat, shop, drink, and listen to tunes at this, the largest one-day festival in South Jersey. Free.

Great Egg Hunt (609-398-4662), Ocean City Beach, between 11th St. and 14th St. Ready, set, go! Five age groups head out onto the beach in search of 20,000 eggs. Happy hunting! Free.

Woofin' Paws Pet Fashion Show (609-399-2629), Ocean City boardwalk. Dress your pup in his or her Easter best for this annual parade.

May

Martin Z. Mollusk Day (609-399-1412), Ocean City Beach at 9th St. Forget that groundhog; in Ocean City it's a hermit crab that determines if spring is really on its way. Will he see his shadow at this bizarre event, which also involves a sea turtle, llama, and Elvis impersonator? Head to the beach to find out. Free.

Dogs in the Doo Dah Parade

July

Night in Venice (609-525-9300), Ocean City Bay. One of the world's largest boat parades is right in Ocean City. The effect is doubled as the houses along the parade route light up to match the procession on the water traveling from the bay and down Tennessee Avenue. It's been an Ocean City tradition since the 19th century, though in its original form it was less merriment and more a showcase-on-water for local debutantes. You can watch from the grandstands lined up along the parade route, finagle an invitation to a bay-side house party, or watch from the Bay Center (for a small fee). Free.

August

Annual Baby Parade (609-525-9300), Ocean City boardwalk at the Music Pier. How cute is your kid, really? Let him or her dazzle the crowd at this parade, which is one of the oldest baby parades in the country. Free.

Boardwalk Art Show (609-399-7628; oceancityartscenter.org), Ocean City boardwalk. This annual art show is one of Ocean City's oldest annual events, and it changes every year depending on who's coming to display their wares. Free.

Miss Crustacean Hermit Crab Beauty Pageant (609-525-9300), Ocean City Beach at 6th St. Watch as these beauties claw their way to the crown. The winner takes the Coveted Cucumber Rind Cup and showcases her beauty by crawling her way down a flowery runway. Stick around because the day after the pageant are hermit crab races, also on the 6th Street Beach. Free.

Weird Week (609-525-9300), Ocean City boardwalk at the Music Pier. They're not kidding when they call this weird week. You have to see it to believe how weird it can be. Events start at 11 AM every weekday, and culminate with the crowning of Mr. and Miss Miscellaneous. Free.

October

Hayrides on the Boardwalk (609-398-4662), Ocean City boardwalk. That's right—you can get your hayride with a dash of salt air thrown in. They provide free pumpkins and face painting as well. Free.

Indian Summer Weekend (609-525-9300), Ocean City Music Pier. You'll stuff your stomach and empty your wallet at this three-day festival. Seafood vendors take over the Music Pier, and Asbury Avenue turns into a block party with foods, crafts, music, and plenty of stuff to do. Free.

December

First Night New Year's Eve Celebration (609-525-9300; firstnightocnj.com). Ring in the New Year at this family-friendly (and dry) New Year's Eve celebration, topped off with midnight fireworks. $$.

Important Info
Where to turn when you
need to know

In an emergency, dial 911.
Poison information: 800-222-1222.
Non-emergency fire: 609-525-9182.
Non-emergency police: 609-399-
9111.

HOSPITALS

Shore Memorial Hospital (609-391-8105; shorememorial.org), 914 Haven
Ave., Ocean City 08226.
Shore Memorial Hospital (609-653-3500; shorememorial.org), 1 E. New
York Ave., Somers Point 08244.

NEWSPAPERS

Ocean City Gazette (609-624-8900; oceancitygazette.com).
Ocean City Sentinel (609-399-5411).
The Sandpaper Magazine (609-624-8900; oceancitygazette.com/sp).

REALTORS

Ocean City Board of Realtors (609-399-0128; ocbor.com), 405 22nd St.,
Ocean City 08226.

TRANSPORTATION

Action Transportation (609-839-9797).
C&C Cab Company (609-399-9100).
Gerry's A-1 Transportation (609-399-7444 and 609-927-9140).
Enterprise Rent-A-Car (609-390-1061; enterprise.com).
Just Four Wheels (609-399-2522; just4wheels.com).

TOURISM CONTACTS

Ocean City Chamber of Commerce (609-399-1412; oceancityvacation
.com).
Ocean City Tourism Commission (800-BEACH-NJ; njoceancity.com).
New Jersey Travel and Tourism (800-VISITNJ; state.nj.us/travel).

3

Sea Isle City

VACATIONERS' DELIGHT

Including Strathmere

HISTORY

CHARLES K. LANDIS was so smitten with Italy that when he returned home, he decided to re-create it. He bought the area that is now Sea Isle City, making it a borough by 1880.

Sea Isle City might not look anything like an Italian resort now, but a few of those 1880s buildings are still around, and people still vacation here. In droves.

It's located on a narrow barrier island bordered by the Atlantic Ocean on the east and marsh on the west. The more southerly streets are popular with families who come to town to enjoy the beach, the water, and the seafood joints.

Sea Isle is also a spot for 20- and 30-somethings who fill the cluster of bars in the 30s and 40s streets around Landis Avenue. They don't come for the week, but rent houses with 15 of their closest friends and jam up those bars on summer weekends. You won't find many hotels, motels, or bed & breakfasts here; most people rent private houses or condos for their week-long stay.

Sea Isle has plenty of family-friendly restaurants, from oceanside pizza parlors to cafés, no jackets required. You can also rock out to cover bands and pick up "a slice" at 2 AM—all this within blocks.

Sea Isle shares the island with Strathmere, its northern neighbor. It's a slip of a town that has a handful of restaurants and bars and far smaller crowds than Sea Isle. It's still a relatively unknown patch of the Jersey Shore, and has managed to stave off overdevelopment. Even though it isn't

LEFT: The author's dog, Emily, on the beach in Strathmere

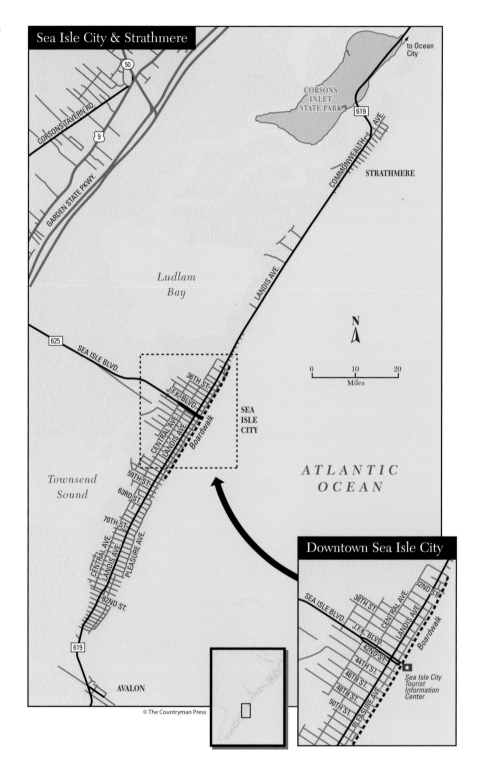

Sea Isle City & Strathmere

to Ocean City

CORSONS INLET STATE PARK

STRATHMERE

COMMONWEALTH AVE.

619

CORSONS TAVERN RD.

50

9

GARDEN STATE PKWY.

Ludlam Bay

LANDIS AVE.

625

SEA ISLE BLVD.

N

0   10   20
Miles

36TH ST.

J.F.K. BLVD.

CENTRAL AVE.

LANDIS AVE.

Boardwalk

SEA ISLE CITY

59TH ST.

63RD ST.

Townsend Sound

70TH ST.

CENTRAL AVE.

LANDIS AVE.

PLEASURE AVE.

ATLANTIC OCEAN

82ND ST.

619

AVALON

© The Countryman Press

Downtown Sea Isle City

SEA ISLE BLVD.

38TH ST.

32ND ST.

CENTRAL AVE.

LANDIS AVE.

Boardwalk

J.F.K. BLVD

42ND ST.

44TH ST.

46TH ST.

PLEASURE AVE.

48TH ST.

50TH ST.

★ Sea Isle City Tourist Information Center

Sisters of Mercy   Courtesy of James T. Hoffman

technically allowed, people bring their dogs to this beach. No one's there to say no.

Whether you're bringing the family or looking for casual shore bars—or both—Sea Isle City could have what you're looking for. No promises on a gondola running down Landis Avenue anytime soon.

Pick Your Spot

Best places to stay in and around Sea Isle City

Coast Motel (609-263-3756; lacosta-seaisle.com), 4000 Landis Ave., Sea Isle City 08243. This motel, which is half a block from the beach and smack in the center of town, is a drop-your-stuff-and-go kind of place. That's not to say it's a bad choice when it comes to where to stay. The 33 rooms at the Coast are clean and well maintained, with their own kitchenettes. Open in-season. $$.

The Colonnade Inn (609-263-8868; thecolonnadeinn.com), 4600 Landis Ave., Sea Isle City 08243. When the Jersey Shore started receiving visitors, the Colonnade Inn—built around 1883—was one of the many resorts catering to them. Today it's the only hotel from that era standing in Sea Isle. In 2004, it was restored to its original splendor, which shows in each of its 19 lodging options. They come in one-, two-, and three-room suites. The Colonnade operates much in the way a bed & breakfast does, except many of the rooms belong to private owners who rent out their space when they're not in Sea Isle City. Don't skip the porch views. You'll see everything going on in the center of town. $$–$$$.

DiGenni's Centennial Guest House (609-263-6945; centennial guesthouse.com), 127 39th St., Sea Isle City 08243. This is a house with a past. DiGenni's Centennial Guest House was built in 1885 as a summer home for a wealthy Philadelphian. During Prohibition, it became a speakeasy. John and Madge DiGenni bought the house in 1980 and renamed it the Centennial Guest House in 1982 in honor of Sea Isle City's 100th birthday. John DiGenni, the couple's son, now runs it. There is no breakfast (it's not a B&B), and the rooms don't have private bath. But they are clean, charming, and come with air-conditioning and wireless Internet. Make sure to bring your own towels. Open in-season. $–$$.

Local Flavors

Taste of the town—local restaurants, cafés, bars, bistros, etc.

Braca's Café (609-263-4271; braca cafe.com), 18 JFK Blvd., Sea Isle City 08243. *Braca* was stamped all over Sea Isle City starting in 1901, when Lou and Madelena Braca moved here. There was a barbershop, grocery store, real estate company, theater, gift and card shop, ice cream store, and bowling alley, all with the *Braca* name. Many of the businesses were destroyed by storms, but Braca's Café still thrives in what used to be the Braca family home. The menu offers surf-and-turf options with a hearty dose of pasta meals. The crowd turns more bar-hopping later at night. Make sure to try a 302. It's a frozen concoction that goes down smoothly after a day on the beach—but you've been warned: It's powerful. Dinner; lunch Fri.–Sun. $$–$$$.

Dead Dog Saloon (609-263-7600; seaislenightlife.com), 3809 Landis Ave., Sea Isle City 08243. They're not kidding about the dress code. Guys, if you walk in wearing a T-shirt, you are required to put down a $10 deposit on a Dead Dog Saloon collared shirt (and if you "forget" to return the shirt, it's yours, and they keep your $10). No baseball hats are allowed, either, in the evening. The menu is strictly bar food, but good bar food with items like personal pizzas, coconut shrimp, and potstickers—shrimp or pork folded into a pastry with vegetables. The music and entertainment are usually low-key, even on the busier summer weekends. No credit cards, though there's an ATM on site. Dinner plus lunch on Sat. and Sun. in-season. $.

Deauville Inn (609-263-2080; deauvilleinn.com), 201 Willard Rd., Strathmere 08248. They say the sunsets are complimentary at the Deauville Inn, which straddles the border of Ocean City and Strathmere. They aren't to be missed, especially in the warmer months when you can sit dockside for lunch, dinner, or a late-night snack, or enjoy your drinks on the sand where the motto is "No shoes, no shirt, no problem." As to be expected at a bay-side eatery, the menu is dominated by seafood. Reservations are recommended for dinner if you want to eat inside. Lunch, dinner, late night in-season. Closed Tue.–Wed. from Oct. to Apr. $$$.

Dock Mike's Pancake House (609-263-3625; dock-mikes.com), 4615 Landis Ave., Sea Isle City 08243. The name here is misleading. While Dock Mike's dishes up pancakes in many different varieties, including sweet potato and "Mikey" Mouse, it's also a lunch spot and has more than 100 different items to try, like wraps, seafood samplers, and cheese steaks, all of which are listed on your place-mat menu. No credit cards. Breakfast, lunch. $–$$.

Giovanni's Deli and Sub Shop (609-263-7684), 4309 Landis Ave., Sea Isle City 08243. If you can't tell this is a true Italian

Dock Mike's

Busch's

(609-263-8626; buschsseafood.com), 8700 Anna Phillips Lane, Sea Isle City 08243. Long live Busch's! This beloved classic seafood restaurant was supposed to celebrate its final year in 2010, more than 125 years after its opening. But the condo development deal for the site fell through, so this favorite will be back in 2011—at least. Pick from the wealth of sea-themed meals, or try two at once—like baked deviled crabs and fried scallops—via Busch's combo entrées. The one thing you cannot skip is the she-crab soup. Owner Al Schettig makes it himself, by himself, to ensure that his recipe stays a secret. Dinner in-season. Closed Mon. $$.

deli by the tins of extra-virgin olive oil lined up in the window, you will when you walk in and are hit with that spicy meat-and-cheese smell. The hoagies are the main attraction, though they also stock deli meats and cheeses, plus pre-cooked meals and sides, like antipasto, salads, and Italian cookies. If you're making your own Italian masterpiece, Giovanni's also stocks everything you'll need, from the pasta to the sauce to that extra-virgin olive oil. Lunch, dinner. $.

Lobster Loft (609-263-3000), 318 42nd Place, Sea Isle City 08243. Hard to miss the Lobster Loft when you're driving into Sea Isle—there's a giant red lobster on the building. They dish up excellent pastas and seafood. Sit at the downstairs back bar if you can—they usually run food specials, like half-price appetizers. The bar scene at night is more grown-up than what you'll find at the cover-band bars, though you'll sometimes find them at the Lobster Loft, too. Dinner. $$$.

McGowan's Food Market and Deli (609-263-5500), 3900 Landis Ave., Sea Isle City 08243. If you stop for a sandwich at only one place in Sea Isle, make it McGowan's. Their sandwiches are so big and stuffed with, well, stuff that you'll be full through dinner. They're popular for their breakfast dishes, too. It's all take-out. They have a mini mart section in case you need more than just sandwiches and sodas for sustenance. No credit cards. Breakfast, lunch in-season. $.

Mike's Seafood (609-263-4342; mikesseafood.com), 4222 Park Rd., Sea Isle City 08243. You can take out seafood from this spot, which celebrated its 100th anniversary in 2011, or eat on the dock—literally. The dining area is covered with a thick green awning, but the sides are open to the water and air, just enough to give you that outdoor-

Nickelby's

dining feel while staying cool. You can come in a large group and order your crabs by the pound (ready for you to crack and clean on your own if you so choose), or grab one of the smaller tables for two. It's BYO—beer and wine only—and busy on the weekends, so expect a line around dinner-time, though you can have a pre-dinner drink while waiting for your table. Lunch, dinner in-season. Fri.–Sat. 9 AM–7 PM, Sun. 9–5 off-season. $$.

Mrs. Brizzle's (609-263-2773), 4601 Landis Ave., Sea Isle City 08243. The homemade cinnamon buns are only one portion of the missus's eat-in-or-take-out shop. She (or the college kids working behind the counter) also sells breakfast sandwiches, hoagies, and salads. This new location has more indoor seating. No credit cards. Breakfast, lunch. $.

Nickelby's (609-263-1184), 8301 Landis Ave., Sea Isle City 08243. You won't find anything closer to an old-fashioned country store at the shore than Nickelby's, which sits on the meeting point of Landis and East Landis Avenues. A small selection of groceries, toiletries, hats, shirts and toys, a deli and bakery, plus a coffee bar. Cash preferred. Breakfast, lunch in-season. $.

Ocean Drive (609-263-1000; theod.com), 3915 Landis Ave., Sea Isle City 08243. It's not exactly the place where everybody knows your name. It's possible that no one will be able to find you in this always-packed shore tradition of a bar. It's

Crabbing

They're pinchy little buggers, those crabs that live in the back bays and inlets of the Jersey Shore. You have a few options on how to get them from the water to your plate. Here's how, from easiest to most difficult:

1. Order them, prepared into a tasty dish, at a restaurant.

2. Order them cooked whole at a restaurant. This leaves the cracking and cleaning up to you. It's a science if you want to get out every single scrap of meat. My aunt Margie would take everyone's leftovers and pick clean what we couldn't get to. She got at least another crab or two worth of meat out of our scraps. You can buy these kinds of crabs at most seafood shops, or at restaurants like **Mike's Seafood and Raw Bar** (609-263-1136, 222 Park Rd., Sea Isle City 08243), where you can order them by the pound.

3. Buy live crabs, and prepare them at home. This is not for the squeamish, as you'll either have to boil the crabs alive, or kill them (typically by opening their backs) and clean them while they're still squirmy.

4. Catch them. There's two levels of this method, too: the easy way, and the right way. The easy way is to buy or rent a crab trap. You bait it, put in the water, and wait for a crab to walk inside. The right way is to make your own baited lines using rope, chicken backs, and fishing weights. Throw your line in the water (tied off to a pier or boat) and check it every 5 to 20 minutes, depending on how busy it is that day in the water. Then slowly, very slowly, pull up the line, at just the right speed so the crab doesn't jump off the chicken or even realize that he's moving. Lower a net under the crab-on-bait, and voilà. Dinner.

where the young'uns go in Sea Isle City and has been for the last 30 years. The drinks are cold; the cover bands are loud and play all the songs you know. Don't expect a huge drink selection—bottled beer and whatever the shot girl offers. No one will scoff if you come right off the beach. Expect daytime crowds on weekends in-season for No Shower Happy Hour and Sun-day Funday events. Lunch, dinner, late night in-season. Call for off-season hours. They typically open for off-season holiday weekends. $.

O'Donnell's Pour House (609-263-5600), 3907 Landis Ave., Sea Isle City 08234. It's mostly fish, meat, and classic Irish dishes at this small eatery, but what really draws the patrons is the drink menu, specifically the whiskey. You can get

I spent more than a few August days out on a one-engine boat, lines in the water, waiting for a crab to bite that chicken back. Every year when my grandparents, cousins, aunts, and uncles would join my family at the shore, we'd rent boats from Landis Marina in Sea Isle and catch dinner.

My grandfather Anthony Verzella taught me how to tie on the chicken back while weighing down the line, and how to time the net just right so that the crab won't dance away. I've seen him pinched by a crab, too, and not even wince. He was a big man, solid as an oak tree, a World War II vet and former construction superintendent with huge hands. A little crab wasn't going to bother him.

After a full day on the boat, we'd bring our catch back to where we were staying and my mother, grandmother, and aunts would build a huge crab feast around pastas and garlic bread, salads and corn on the cob.

My grandfather passed away while I was writing and researching the first edition of this book. As I helped my mom clean out my grand-parents' house, I found an AAA guide from 1988 about RV and tent sites in the mid-Atlantic. Tucked inside were newspaper articles about where to go to catch the best crabs and a place mat from a seafood joint that had step-by-step, illustrated instructions on how to best clean the meat.

When my cousins grew up and stopped coming down the shore every summer, my mom and aunts started buying the crabs instead—live—and creating the feast. It was cheaper, cleaner, and quicker than renting boats. But I miss the chase and those lazy days on a boat with my grandfather, waiting for the next big catch.

cold beers, too, and it's one of the few relatively unpacked-to-the-gills spots around where you can watch baseball games in-season. Lunch, dinner in-season. $$.

Springfield Inn (609-263-4951; thespringfieldinn.com), 8 43rd St., Sea Isle City 08243. "The Spring-field," as it's more commonly known, isn't really an inn. It's a cen-ter for live music and cold drinks,

skewing older in age than the crowd that flocks to Ocean Drive. The Springfield also has one of the few beach bars in the area—the Carousel, which also has live music (and not a carousel in sight). The view is more boardwalk than beach, but a seat at the under-cabana bar is relaxing just the same. $.

Sweet Pete's (609-263-1116), 6116 Landis Ave., Sea Isle City

Bar at the Carousel

08243. It's hard not to feel cheery in this candy-striped ice cream parlor, which also dishes up yummy desserts for everyone and coffee drinks for the grown-ups. Try one of their specialty sundaes, like Mint Explosion or Strawberry Shortcake. You can't go wrong with the tradi-tional banana split, either. No credit cards. Lunch, dinner in-season. $.

Twisties (609-263-2200; twist iestavern.com), 232 Bayview Dr., Strathmere 08248. Their unofficial tag line is "Find us if you can!" It's a bit of a hunt, but once you locate this bar on the bay, you might not want to leave. Since 1940, it's been the place to drink overlooking the marsh in Strathmere. Open at noon. Closed Tue. in-season. Open Fri.–Sun. in spring and fall. $.

Valarie's Place (609-263-5400; valariesplace.com), 5900 Landis Ave., Sea Isle City 08243. Expect a good meal in a cozy atmosphere at this restaurant, which not only accepts kids but reaches out to them for breakfast, lunch, and dinner. The walls are decorated with colorful handprints from children who've visited. There's even a play area. The menu leans toward pasta and seafood. Make sure you try the Crab Chowder. BYOB. Breakfast, lunch, dinner. Call for off-season hours. $$.

Yum Yum's Ice Cream (609-263-2345), 31 JFK Blvd., Sea Isle City 08243. You can get just about any kind of ice cream you want at Yum Yum's. You'll have to wait on the weekends, but it's worth it for the treat at the bottom of the cone: a gumdrop. It started as a way to keep ice cream from leaking out and has stayed because it gives your cone a little something extra. No credit cards. Open noon–11:30 PM in-season (or later if the crowds keep coming). $.

Don't Miss This

Check out these great attractions and activities . . .

Book Nook (609-263-1311), 3800 Boardwalk, Sea Isle City 08243. This boardwalk bookstore is an ideal place to grab beach reading material. They have magazine racks in the front and back of the store (the front is more "greatest hits" of what's popular on the beach), plus the mysteries, thrillers, and deep reads that'll keep you anchored to your beach chair. They've also dedicated a chunk of the store to children's books and activity books to keep the younger members of your group occupied. Open 9 AM–10 PM in-season.

Chrissie's Boutique (609-263-3509), 3806 Landis Ave, Sea Isle City 08243. You'll find dresses of all kinds, from floaty cotton sundresses to bombshell satin halter-top gowns, and not for outrageous prices. The store is nearly as charming as the dresses themselves. Clothes are displayed on the porch and draped inside this 19th-century building. Open 9:30 AM–9:30 PM.

Coffee.COMedy (609-263-JAVA; coffeedotcomedy.com), 29 JFK Blvd., Sea Isle City 08243. No, this store isn't closed—the windows are tinted to keep it cool, and to provide a better work space for the stand-up comedians who perform at night. Coffee.COMedy serves an array of caffeine-infused drinks since it doubles as a coffeehouse during the day, along with breakfast bagels, sandwiches, and wraps. It has plenty of work-space tables and wireless Internet if you're dying to get some work done. BYOB for comedy shows. Open 7:30 AM–10 PM. Shows start at 9 PM. $.

Dalrymple's (609-263-3337), 20 JFK Blvd., Sea Isle City 08243. It's okay if you can't pronounce the name of this shop—I still can't. It's part Hallmark gift store and part bookstore with a dash of general store thrown in for all those beach-extras you can't live without. The book section stocks a lot of local-interest titles, and the hottest beach reads of the year. Open 7 AM–10 PM in-season. Call for off-season hours.

Gillian's Funland of Sea Isle City (609-263-1363; gillians.com/fun land.asp), 304 JFK Blvd., Sea Isle City 08243. Take the kids to Gillian's Funland for a few thrills and spills. Don't expect high-octane, daredevil rides here, though some might spin you to the point that your dinner is in danger. Open in-season; call for hours, as they vary per week. $–$$.

Haven (609-486-6437; ihearthaven.com), 4105 Landis Ave., Sea Isle City 08243. This boutique leans more toward comfy luxury than beachwear. The styles are very now and hip for the 20- and 30-something set but still casual enough to fit in at the local nightlife scene. They stock tanks, dresses, and jeans, as well as casual sandals, sneakers, and jewelry. Open 10 AM–9 PM.

Heritage Surf & Sport (609-263-3033; heritagesurf.com), 3700 Landis Ave., Sea Isle City 08243. The talk here is all surf all the time—except when mentions of snowboarding or "where I went last night" are thrown in by the staff, who know their surf and know their boards. Heritage also sells surf-

Welcome to Sea Isle City   Courtesy of Marc Steiner/Agency New Jersey

Shoobie

What is a shoobie? You'll hear the locals throw this term around, especially if you're visiting in summer.

Lore has it that locals called day-trippers shoobies because they used to come down for the day and bring their lunch in shoeboxes. I haven't seen anyone bring food down the shore in the shoebox, but the name stuck.

It's not meant as a term of endearment. Locals rejoice when the shoobies go home after Labor Day. The pace slows back down to normal, and you can find parking!

inspired fashions for men, women, and kids. Don't skip the upstairs "board room"—and by *board* I mean surf, snow, and skate. Group and private surf lessons are available. They also stock Uggs and Toms shoes. Open 9 AM–9 PM in-season and 10–6 off-season.

Pirate Island Golf (609-263-8344; pirateislandgolf.com), 33rd St. & Landis Ave., Sea Isle City 08243. Arrrrr, mateys! Belly up to this pirate-ship mini golf course if you dare. The course has enough hazards and traps that it's challenging to even the most seasoned mini golf pros. Open 9 AM–11:30 PM in-season.

Sea Isle City Historical Museum (609-263-2992; jerseyseashore.com/sic_museum/sic_museum.htm), 4208 Landis Ave., Sea Isle City 08243. There was a time when Sea Isle City wasn't overrun by beach rental houses, pizza shops, bars, and shoobies. Those times are reconstructed and celebrated at the Sea Isle City Historical Museum, which has an extensive selection of memorabilia and photos from more than 100 years of Sea Isle City history. Open 10 AM–3 PM Mon., Wed., and Fri.; 10–1 Tue., Thu., and Sat. during summer; 10–1 PM Sat. only Sept.–Dec. and Apr.–June. Special appointments also available in the off-season.

Sea Isle Parasail (609-263-5555; seaisleparasail.com), 86th St. & The Bay, Sea Isle City 08243. Even if you're flying high above the ocean, parasailing is far from a roller-coaster ride, which is why it's open to kids, adults, and seniors (the youngest they've flown here was five years old). Fly solo or with a pal—either way, it's a great way to take in the sights of the Jersey shore. In-season. $$$$.

Sea Isle Watersports Center (609-263-9100; seaislewatersports.com), 329 43rd St., Sea Isle City 08243. For some extra fun on the water, head here to rent a WaveRunner or kayak. They also provide a separated wave-running area, plus guided back-bay tours. Sea Isle Watersports Center

Sessoms Nautical Gifts

stores and winterizes personal watercraft, and services, repairs, and sells used ones, too. Check their website for coupons toward rentals. Open 9 AM–sunset in-season. $$$.

Sessoms Nautical Gifts (609-263-6088), 3800 Boardwalk, Sea Isle 08243. The only requirement for something sold at Sessoms is that it has to do with the ocean—any ocean. Nautical flags, horseshoe crabs, decorative light rings, and shell chandeliers hang from the ceiling and are mixed in

Sea Isle City Promenade

The Promenade in Sea Isle

The boardwalk in Sea Isle doesn't have any boards and isn't even called a boardwalk (even if addresses along the Promenade are still listed as "Boardwalk").

It's not as developed as its counterparts in Atlantic City, Ocean City, and Wildwood, but it's still far from empty. You'll find shops, casual eateries, and amusements along the Promenade. Its intersection with JFK Boulevard hosts a lot of activities, like live bands and performances.

with wooden ships, Pacific island decor, replica pirate booty, and lobster buoys from Maine (that have SEA ISLE written on them). It's a wacky seafaring delight. Open 10 AM–10 PM in-season. Call for off-season hours.

Uncle Al's (609-263-7485), 35th St. & the Boardwalk, Sea Isle City 08243. Test your luck and wooden-ball-throwing skills at one of Uncle Al's 10 skee-ball lanes. If this isn't your game, you can also try other ticket-wining amusements, like slot machines, or play pinball or video games. The prizes you get aren't always top-of-the-line, but it's the journey that's the fun here. Open 10 AM–10 PM in-season. $.

48 Hours

DAY 1

Start out with a big breakfast at Dock Mike's, which has knockout pancake and omelet menus. Not quite in the mood to hit the beach? How about renting a WaveRunner from the Sea Isle Watersports Center?

Then take a bike ride up the island to Strathmere and have lunch with your feet in the (bay) sand at the Deauville—or if you're not bringing kids along, a drink at Twisties (yes, if you can find it).

Post-lunch, take a stroll down Landis Avenue and hit the shops along the way: Chrissie's for dresses, Heritage for surf gear or surf-inspired clothing, Dalrymple's for everything you forgot to bring. Then it's time for dinner at Mike's if the weather is good. Make sure you BYO and are prepared to wait in line if it's a nice summer day (and you can drink while waiting in line).

Now it's time for another stroll, this time up onto the Promenade where the kids can play skee-ball at Uncle Al's, or you can watch the bands that play in-season. If you've got kids, cap your night off with a cone from Yum Yum's—don't forget that there's a gumdrop in the bottom. Of course you can stop there even without kids along, but your nightcap will probably be of a different type.

You must do the Ocean Drive—aka the OD—at least once for crowds and cover bands and a people-watching show. If you're looking for a less frantic night, check out O'Donnell's Pour House—especially if you'd like to watch sports while having your pint.

To start out day 2, hit Mrs. Brizzle's for some sticky buns. Then take a sky-high trip above the water with Sea Isle City Parasail. For lunch, have a monster sandwich at McGowan's—another place worth waiting in line for. Hit the Carousel, which isn't really a carousel but an outdoor sandy bar spot that's attached to the Springfield Inn (also not an inn). Make sure to pop your head into the hut of a bar to see what T-shirts they've nailed to the ceiling for the season.

Ready for a workout? Of course you are after all that food. Hit up the free basketball courts for a pickup game or a little one-on-one. Then—after a shower, of course—stop by the Lobster Loft for half-priced appetizers and live music in-season. Don't eat too much, though, because you're going to take a short walk over to Funland to enjoy rides (or watch your kids enjoying them).

Finally, slide onto a stool at Braca's and have a 302. But be prepared to walk home. They're good, strong, and can knock you on your butt, especially given how much fun you've had over the last 48 hours.

Extend Your Stay

If you have more time, try these great places to see and things to do . . .

Head to the south end of the island for a visit to Nickelby's—part deli, part coffee shop, part beach gear shop. You can also test your putting skills at Pirate Island Golf—the kind of course you'll love if you're into golfing around obstacles. History your thing? Check out the Sea Isle City Historical Museum and see what the island used to be like.

Skee-Ball

Skee-ball is a simple game: For a quarter, you get eight chances to roll a ball up a ramp. Rack up points, get tickets that you can turn in for a bouncy ball, a radio, or a stuffed animal. But at the heart of this classic game is the same goal: skee-ball is all about the 50-point high score.

Skee-ball was born in 1909, which is when it was invented and patented by J. D. Estes of Philadelphia. It wasn't exactly what you find on the boardwalks today. It was an outdoor game with 36-foot alleys. In 1928, the alleys were cut to 14 feet, which meant it could be played by more people, and by people of almost any athletic ability.

Today's ramps are between 10 and 13 feet. The size and shape change, plus the price, also helped the game spread in popularity, especially at the Jersey Shore.

Courtesy of Emil R. Salvini

"One of the reasons skee-ball is so popular is that it's akin to bowling, which is already a popular sport," says Angus Kress Gillespie, professor of American Studies at Rutgers University and co-author of *Looking for America on the New Jersey Turnpike*. "Skee-ball is a feasible alternative to a full-length bowling alley. The real estate on a beachfront boardwalk is so expensive in terms of rent that no business could afford a full-scale bowling alley. What you have in effect is miniature bowling, same as miniature golf."

In 1932, Atlantic City hosted the first national Skee-Ball tournament. It spread to other shore towns, and across the country. Skee-ball has even taken center stage in Hollywood, making cameos in the movies *Chasing Amy* and *Dogma*, and appearing in episodes of *The Simpsons* and *SpongeBob SquarePants*. It's stayed a staple of boardwalk amusements for many of the same reasons it was so popular originally—it's affordable, easy to maintain, and it's fun.

"Another part of the appeal of skee-ball is that there is some skill involved and therefore it lends itself to competition," says Gillespie. "The fact that it's competitive works to the proprietors' advantage because people try to outdo one another."

Probably that more so than the tickets and the prizes.

Special Events

Festivals, parties, and happenings down the shore

WEEKLY (IN-SEASON)

Monday

Free Summer Concerts Under the Stars (609-263-TOUR). Listen to some cool tunes at this outdoor concert. Free.

Tuesday

Guided Beach Combing (609-263-9643), Sea Isle City Beach at 29th St. Let the Sea Isle City Environmental Commission show you the ecological wonders of the beach. $.

Farmer's Market, JFK Blvd. & Pleasure Ave. Get your Jersey fresh produce at this weekly, in-season farmer's market. 8 AM–1 PM.

Movies Under the Stars (609-263-TOUR), Sea Isle City Promenade. Check out a kid-friendly movie at this twice-weekly event. Free.

Wednesday

Free Family Night Dance Parties (609-263-TOUR), Sea Isle City Promenade. Boogie on down to the Promenade for this weekly dance party. Free.

Thursday

Movies Under the Stars (609-263-TOUR), Sea Isle City Promenade. Check out a kid-friendly movie at this twice-weekly event. Free.

Guided Beach Combing (609-263-9643), Sea Isle City Beach at 29th St. Let the Sea Isle City Environmental Commission show you the ecological wonders of the beach. $.

YEARLY

February

Polar Bear Plunge (609-263-TOUR), Sea Isle City Beach at 41st St. If your idea of fun is jumping into the frigid ocean, this is the event for you. If not, check out the costume contest or toast the divers at the post-plunge party. $.

March

Ocean Drive Marathon (609-523-0880; odmarathon.com). Take in the shore sites through this spring marathon, which starts in Cape May and ends in Sea Isle City. The course is all on paved roads and boardwalk. If you're not quite up to 26.2 miles, you can also try a 10-miler, a 5k (3.1 miles), or a 1.5-mile fun run and walk. $$$$.

St. Patrick's Day Parade (609-263-4461, ext. 230), Landis Ave., Sea Isle City. Show off your Irish pride (or the love of the Irish) at this annual parade. Free.

April

Easter Program (609-263-0050), 59th St. & Central Ave., Sea Isle City. Put on your Easter best for this annual parade. Free.

June

Paws on the Promenade (609-390-7946), Sea Isle City Promenade. If you think your dog is just the cutest thing in the world, let him or her stroll on the Sea Isle City boardwalk to show off his or her chops . . . er, paws. Free.

July

Beach Patrol Mascot Races (609-263-3655), Sea Isle City Beach. Little guys and gals who want to be lifeguards can take two days of classes with the Sea Isle City Beach Patrol, the culmination of which are the Mascot Races held every July. Free.

Veterans Memorial Park

Captain Bill Gallagher Island Run (609-263-3655; lmsports.com/seaisle.htm), Sea Isle City Boardwalk and Beach. This annual 10-mile run, which stretches through Sea Isle City and Strathmere, is a flat course, 7 miles of which are on the beach. Feel your calves are up to it? Register online, or watch from the boardwalk. $$.

September

Fall Family Festival Weekend, Sea Isle City Promenade. Check out a hodgepodge of fun family events at this annual fall weekend event, which includes an antique car show, dance party, dance contest, and sand-sculpting contest. Free.

December

New Year's Eve Fireworks, Sea Isle City Promenade. Kick your New Year off with a bang at this fireworks display. Free.

Important Info

Where to turn when you need to know

EMERGENCY NUMBERS

In an emergency, dial 911.
Poison information: 800-222-1222.
Non-emergency fire: 609-263-4311.
Non-emergency police: 609-263-4311.
Ambulance Corps: 609-263-8686.

HOSPITALS

Cape Regional Medical Center (609-463-2000; caperegional.com), 2 Stone Harbor Blvd., Cape May Courthouse 08210.

NEWSPAPERS

Sea Isle Times (609-967-7710; seaisletimes.com).

REALTORS

Coldwell Banker/Laricks Real Estate (877-SIC-RENT; laricks.com), 4110 Landis Ave., Sea Isle City 08243.
Landis Co., Realtors (888-SEA-ISLE; landisco.com), 6000 Landis Ave., Sea Isle City 08243.

NJ Realty, Inc. (800-648-9316; njrealtysic.com), 4914 Landis Ave., Sea Isle City 08243.

Sea Isle Realty, Inc. (888-848-4948; seaislerealty.com), 5906 Landis Ave., Sea Isle City 08243.

TRANSPORTATION

C&C Cab Company (609-399-9100), 115 13th St., Ocean City 08226.

Enterprise Rent A Car (609-522-1119; enterprise.com).

TOURISM CONTACTS

Greater Sea Isle City Chamber of Commerce (609-263-9090; seaisle chamber.com).

New Jersey Travel and Tourism (800-VISITNJ; state.nj.us/travel).

4

Avalon & Stone Harbor

COOLER BY A MILE

Including Cape May Courthouse and Clermont

HISTORY

IN 1722, AARON LEAMING bought the 7-mile-long barrier island that is now Avalon and Stone Harbor. The two towns are separate municipalities but blend together (I'd have a hard time telling where they change if not for signs at the border). Leaming paid about $380 for the island; today you couldn't buy a piece of sidewalk for that price.

Seven Mile Island has long been a vacation spot for the tonier families of the Philadelphia area—there's a reason the harbors are called Princeton, Yale, and Cornell. A lot of the homes were privately owned cottages kept for families to use on the weekends and maybe a few weeks through the summer for their annual vacation. Some, too,

Stone Harbor beach   Courtesy of Scott Neumyer

were rented out to families and packs of 20- and 30-somethings on summer weekends. The same is true today, but pricier.

Avalon and Stone Harbor mix the family-friendliness of Ocean City and nightlife of Sea Isle and Wildwood with an upscale twist that's grown more pronounced in the last decade as some homes have shot past a $10 million price tag.

LEFT: Stone Harbor beach before a storm   Courtesy of Scott Neumyer

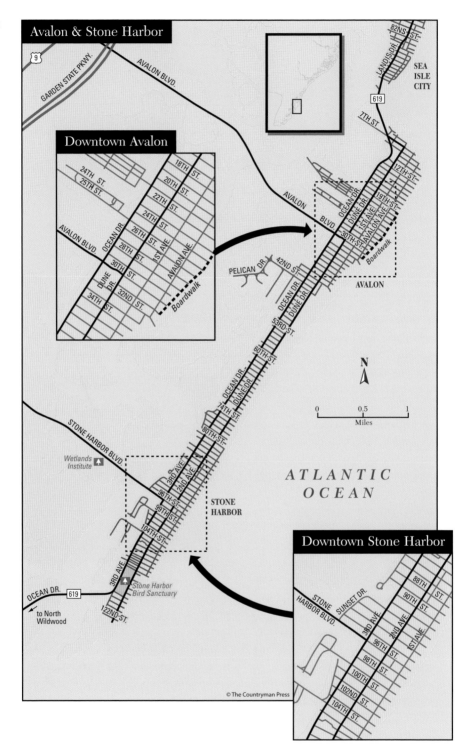

Avalon & Stone Harbor

Downtown Avalon

Downtown Stone Harbor

SEA ISLE CITY

AVALON

STONE HARBOR

ATLANTIC OCEAN

Wetlands Institute

Stone Harbor Bird Sanctuary

to North Wildwood

N

0   0.5   1
Miles

© The Countryman Press

96th Street   Courtesy of Scott Neumyer

Even through the Great Recession, new high-end shopping on Dune Drive in Avalon and 96th Street in Stone Harbor has opened and thrived. Sure, you've still got your bakeries, pastry shops, Italian and seafood restaurants, pizzerias and corner bars, but these days you'll also find gourmet dining, boutique shopping, and a lot more designer labels than you ever saw on the island before.

That's not to say Avalon and Stone Harbor put on airs. The area is a haven for vacationers of all economic levels, and still has a laid-back feel. You'll see families riding bikes, packed beaches, and busy nightlife, usually of the jeans and T-shirt variety. The island also enjoys a prime location in the middle of the South Jersey Shore, putting you between Atlantic City and Cape May if you're looking to explore all the shore towns during your stay.

Renting private homes is still popular, which is why I've included contact information for Realtors at the end of this chapter.

Pick Your Spot

Best places to stay in and around Avalon & Stone Harbor

Colonial Lodge (609-368-2202; stoneharbormotels.com/colonial .htm), 9310 2nd Ave., Stone Harbor 08247. It's quaint and cozy at this brick-faced motel that tips a four-cornered hat to the colonial era, even if the building hasn't been around that long. The rooms are clean and cool—a great place to nap after your beach trip and

before a night on the town. Or you can take advantage of the wide balconies and white tables and chairs on the sundeck. There's also a cottage house for rent next to the motel. Open in-season. $$–$$$.

Concord Suites (800-443-8202; concordsuites.com), 7800 Dune Dr., Avalon 08202. The Concord is the only all-suite hotel in Avalon, and those suites were renovated for the 2010 season. You'll also find two pools and three sundecks if the sand isn't quite your thing. Make sure to stop in the Concord Café for at least one meal while you're in

Colonial Lodge

town. It has some of the best bar food on the island. Open in-season. $$$.

The Golden Inn (609-368-5155; goldeninn.com), 7849 Dune Dr., Avalon 08202. Robert Golden built the Golden Inn in 1961 as a 50-room hotel with a dining room. Today it's a 154-room, beachfront spot run by VF Hotels, which bought the hotel when Golden died in 1983 (they also run spots in Philadelphia, King of Prussia, and Wayne, Pennsylvania). The Golden Inn today is what you'd expect from a place that caters to conferences in the off-season, but next to the beach. Dining on-site is superb. Robert Golden's dining room is still there—and still called the Dining Room—but for a special treat, check out Luigi's Pasta & Vino, a casual Italian restaurant. Free wireless. $$$–$$$$.

Pebbles Guest House (609-368-2203), 9400 1st Ave., Stone Harbor 08247. Pebbles Guest House has the same Victorian

charm that's made Cape May a destination. Built in 1909, it's just three houses from the beach and close to the center of Stone Harbor. The guesthouse has both room and apartments, but not all accommodations have a private bath—remember, it's a guesthouse, not a B&B, so choose carefully if this is a concern. $$–$$$.

Risley House Bed & Breakfast (609-368-1133; risleyhouse.net), 8421 1st Ave., Stone Harbor 08247. The Risley house is as tied to Stone

Peek into Avalon's Past

If you yearn for the cottage days of Avalon, check out avalonspast.com, a website dedicated to how the island used to be. It's run by Dave Coskey, publisher of *7 Mile Times*, the local Avalon newspaper you'll find free in most stores and restaurants.

Avalon Campground

In 1966, Leonard and Connie Catanoso carved a campground from 80 wooded acres off Route 9 in Clermont, New Jersey, just outside Avalon. At about the same time, my grandparents were looking for a place to take their family on vacation. They settled on the campground, rolling up with their camper, eight kids, and a lot of camping gear.

Our family tradition of going to Avalon Campground lasted almost as long as the campground has. I don't even remember when my parents bought our trailer, a tiny slip of a thing that we somehow squeezed six people into on weekends when my father came down the shore. My mother, my three siblings, and I stayed down almost all summer. We lived at the campground, in the pool, in the woods, and on the beach. I learned how to ride my bike on what were then dirt trails, how to do a perfect swan dive, the fine art of shuffle-board, and how to bug the crud out of my younger siblings. On cooler nights, my older brother and I slept on cots in a tent outside. That combination of cot and sleeping bag is still the most comfortable bed I've ever had, though I could live without the skunks walking past us at night.

We sold the trailer when I was 17—my parents divorced, and I was caught up in high school soccer. The trailer itself was falling apart, too. We hadn't bought it new. Then it was just easier to rent a house in Sea Isle for a week than to hike back to the woods and cramp everyone into one small space.

Leonard and Connie don't run the campground anymore. They retired to Florida, but two of their children, Marlene Testa and Lenny Cataonoso Jr., run the show. The roads are paved now, the clubhouse has an Internet café, and not many people use the pay phones—but otherwise this campground is almost exactly the same. I hope that if I'm lucky enough to have kids of my own, I'll continue the tradition for them, shooing them up to the pool so I can cook dinner over an open fire, or walking them to the big field to look up at the stars against an impossibly black sky.

Harbor as the name of the town. Reese Risley, one of the three brothers who founded and governed Stone Harbor, built the Risley House in the early 1900s. In the late 1990s it underwent a major renovation to bring it up to modern standards while retaining its Victorian appeal, especially in the rooms, which have that charm but without the over-the-top Victorian fuss that can turn off some travelers. Pre-renovation, it was called the Holiday Manor Guest House. Closed in winter. $$–$$$.

Sea Lark Bed & Breakfast (609-967-5647; sealark.com), 3018 1st Ave., Avalon 08202. The Sea Lark is the only bed & breakfast in Avalon. The furniture has been passed down through the innkeepers' family. If you're an art fan, rent the Artist's Loft, a third-floor room decorated with works by a friend of the owners. It has a big deck if you're less into art and more into sun. Open in-season. $$–$$$.

Windrift Hotel (800-453-7438; windrifthotel.com), 125 80th St., Avalon 08202. The Windrift, a beach-side Avalon staple, recently had a face-lift, bringing a touch more class to an old favorite. The rooms range from efficiencies to three-bedroom condos. You can also eat and drink by the pool and sundeck. Open in-season and in Sept.; weekends in Oct. $$$–$$$$.

Local Flavors

Taste of the town—local restaurants, cafés, bars, bistros, etc.

Avalon Freeze (609-967-4141), 23rd & Dune Dr., Avalon 08202. Since the 1950s, Avalon Freeze has been capping vacationers' nights with something sweet. Soft-serve rules here, though they do have other ice cream and yogurt options. Open noon–11 PM in-season.

Avalon Seafood & Produce Market (609-967-7555; avalon seafood.com), 2909 Dune Dr., Avalon 08202. Get what's fresh from the land and sea at this seafood and produce market. They sell what-ever's coming in off the farms (the Jersey Shore is close to the farms that put the *Garden* in *Garden State*), plus gourmet salads, dips, and salsa. On the seafood side, they stock whatever you might want from the sea, including scallops, fish, lobster tails, shrimp, crab, and clams. Buy fresh or in one of their platters. It's all take-out. Don't skip dessert, either—they have a pastry chef on site. Seafood market open 10 AM–9 PM and produce market open 8 AM–9 PM, May–Oct. $$.

Back Bay Seafood (609-368-2022; backbayseafood.net), 8305 3rd Ave., Stone Harbor 08247. Their slogan is "Our Fish Slept in the Ocean Last Night," and they aren't kidding. Everything is as fresh as you can get. Pick up the uncooked stuff—no reservation required. If you want the folks at Back Bay to make up their signature crabcakes, lobster tails, shrimp, scallops, and fish dishes, call ahead for a time slot or you'll be left without dinner. Open 11 AM–9 PM in-season. $$.

The Back Yard (609-368-2627), 220 81st St., Stone Harbor 08247. You might forget your shore location at the Back Yard. It's set in a magical garden that includes a grape arbor. The menu is small but sophisticated, and you can trust the chef's instincts. Reservations recommended. BYOB. Dinner in-season. $$$.

Bobby Dee's Rock 'n Chair (609-967-3300; rocknchair.net), 2409 Dune Dr., Avalon 08202. You won't find a more established local tradition than dinner at the Rock 'n Chair. The food is upscale but in a laid-back setting. Upstairz at the Chair is the more casual portion of the bar. Rock 'n Chair is open year-round; Upstairz, in-season. Lunch, dinner, late night. $$–$$$$.

Brady's Hoagie Dock (609-368-8213), 6740 Ocean Dr., Avalon 08202. Don't know what a hoagie is? You'll learn at this shop, which is situated away from the crowds of downtown Avalon. You might call it

Avalon Freeze   Courtesy of Scott Neumyer

Brian's Waffle House   Courtesy of Scott Neumyer

a sub or a hero, but here, it's all hoagie. Each sandwich is packed with provolone cheese, lettuce, tomatoes, and onions, then with whatever meat guts you like—tuna, Italian ham, roast beef, chicken salad. Brady's also sells wings, burgers, chicken, steak sandwiches, and salads. Lunch, dinner in-season. Lunch off-season. $.

Bread and Cheese Cupboard (609-368-1135), 246 96th St., Stone Harbor 08247. For more than 30 years, this little shop with the orange awning has lured customers inside with the sweet smell wafting out the front door. Sure, they sell breads and cheeses, birthday cakes and coffees, but it's the sticky buns that are the prized menu item. Get them with raisins or walnuts—or without. Just don't skimp on the syrup. It's what puts the *sticky* in

the *sticky buns*. No credit cards. Open 7 AM–6 PM in-season. $.

Brian's Waffle House (609-967-3058), 2408 Dune Dr., Avalon 08202. It's all breakfast all the time at this busy waffle house—which also, of course, sells other breakfast items, like pancakes, omelets, and cereal. Their multigrain waffles are as tasty as the not-so-healthy variety. Don't let the long lines outside deceive you. Brian's is bigger inside than it looks, with waits shorter than you'd expect, unless you're vying for one of the few outdoor tables. No credit cards. Breakfast, lunch until 2 PM. $.

Café Loren (609-967-8228; cafeloren.com), 2288 Dune Dr., Avalon 08202. Café Loren dishes up classic American cuisine in a casual setting (though they do ask that gentlemen wear collared

How to Eat a Sticky Bun from the Bread and Cheese Cupboard

1. Do not let anyone offer to pick them up for you. You need to be in control of all sticky bun decisions, and if you don't go yourself, you can't revel in the syrup and cinnamon scents that fill this Stone Harbor bakery.

2. Buy half a dozen, at least, even if only one or two people say they're interested. Buy the sticky buns with raisins on top. It makes them much more interesting, and you can argue that you're eating the sticky buns for the fruit. No one, however, will believe you.

3. Once you return with your package, set the box on the counter, open the lid, and breathe deeply. Even if you picked them up from the shop, one more hit of the sticky bun smell will properly whet your appetite.

4. Choose a bun from the middle. This will ensure that you get four sides of soft, sweet dough.

5. Using your hands, pick up a bun, and bite. Savor. Chew. Lick fingers. Repeat.

6. Lick all remaining syrup off your fingers.

7. Hide the remaining sticky buns in the microwave.

8. Repeat steps 5–7 throughout the day. Do not let buns sit overnight, and never *ever* try to freeze them for later consumption. Fresh, right from the baker's oven, is best.

shirts). You can go with the Café Loren tried and true, like the grilled lobster tail, grilled pork tenderloin, or grilled filet mignon, or try one of chef-owner Stephen Serano's daily menu additions. BYOB. Dinner in-season. Closed Mon. $$$.

Circle Pizza (609-967-7566; avalonpizza.com), 2108 Dune Dr., Avalon 08202. This has been a popular pizza spot for more than 40 years, especially among late-night bar-hoppers looking for a snack.

The menu, which you can eat in or take out, leans heavily on pizza but also includes sandwiches and a surprisingly diverse salad selection. Lunch, dinner, late night. $.

Circle Tavern at the Princeton (609-967-3456; princetonbar.com), 2008 Dune Dr., Avalon 08202. The Princeton, aka "the P," is the place to end your night if you like to have a few drinks and dance to cover bands or top 40 hits. You either love or hate the crowds, the noise, and the high levels of alcohol intake. But that's not to detract from the Circle Tavern portion of the Princeton, which is open year-round and does a good job dishing up quality lunch and dinner items. The Burger-Bomb—an apple-smoked burger with bacon, mushrooms, and cheese—is a tasty flip on an old classic. You're best served getting out of there before 9 PM in-season, which is when the bar crowd starts flocking in, if you're looking for a relaxing meal. Lunch, dinner, late night. $$.

Coffee Talk (609-368-5282), 299 96th St., Stone Harbor 08247. Caffeinate yourself at this coffeehouse and restaurant. The decor is an eclectic mix, from the turquoise vinyl diner booths to the velour fainting chair. Tables come with playing cards and checkerboards.

No credit cards. Open breakfast, lunch in-season. Call for off-season hours. $.

Concord Café (609-368-5505; concordcafe.net), Concord Suites, 7800 Dune Dr., Avalon 08202. This is where the locals go, and I don't blame them. The Concord Café has knockout bar food. Create your own burger or make a meal of the bar foods. The fries doused in Buffalo wing sauce and crumbled blue cheese is enough for two—and my favorite menu item. It's a small place that's always packed in summer, so prepare to wait, or grab one of the few seats at the bar. Lunch, dinner in-season. $.

The Diving Horse (609-368-5000; thedivinghorseavalon.com), 2109 Dune Dr., Avalon 08202. The Diving Horse is the brainchild of

The Diving Horse   Courtesy of the Diving Horse

What Is *In-Season*?

When I write *in-season*, I generally mean the time between Memorial Day weekend (late May) and Labor Day weekend (early September), but in reality each venue has its own version. Many shore spots start their season by being open on weekends starting Mother's Day, and/or extend the season through September. But some places, like Springer's Homemade Ice Cream, shut down on Labor Day, no exceptions. If you're staying in the spring or fall shoulder season and really want to stop at one of the places I say is open in-season, your best bet is to call first.

three successful Philadelphia restaurateurs with ties to the Jersey Shore. Dan Clark, Ed Hackett, and chef Jonathan Adams opened this BYOB seafood spot as a place to serve locally sourced foods, which is why the menu changes almost every night depending on what's in-season. Reservations are a must. The restaurant only seats 70. BYOB. Dinner in-season. $$$$.

Green Cuisine (609-368-1616), 302 96th St., Stone Harbor 08247. Healthy food alert! The menu at Green Cuisine is hearty but healthy with pita sandwiches, salads, wraps, and salad options. The Greek pita is my favorite—the feta, olives, veggies, and sprouts stuffed into a whole wheat pita has hit the spot more than once. They have a in-house smoothie bar, too. It gets crowded, so there's a stack of magazines to keep you occupied if the wait is too long. No credit cards. Lunch, dinner in-season. $.

Maggie's (609-368-7422), 2619 Dune Dr., Avalon 08202. The NO WHINING shirts aren't directed at you. Maggie always said this to her grandchildren, so they put it on the shirt. The dining is casual during the day (classic breakfast and lunch foods, plus an excellent grilled-cheese menu), but the tables are draped with linens at night to class things up. Maggie's runs a free book swap, too, if you're looking for a good beach read and have one to share. Breakfast, lunch, dinner. $–$$.

Mallon's (609-967-5400; mallonsbakery.com), 2105 Ocean Dr., Avalon 08202. If you like sticky buns, this is your spot. Mallon's makes 14 flavors of this gooey treat. They also sell other fresh-made sweet breakfast treats, like homemade doughnuts, muffins, and crumb cake, plus bagels, cookies, and coffee. No credit cards. Open daily 7 AM–1 PM mid-June–Labor Day; weekends only in spring and fall. $.

The Sea Grill (609-967-5511; seagrillrestaurant.com), 225 21st St., Avalon 08202. There's no set menu at the Sea Grill. Instead, check out what sea and land items are offered that day by reading the blackboard, and tell the chef what you'd like and how you want it cooked. Don't skip the artwork. All of those funky paintings are from the owners' private collection. The Sea Grill also has an extensive wine list with nightly wine specials. $$$.

Springer's Homemade Ice Cream (609-368-4631; springersice cream.com), 9420 3rd Ave., Stone Harbor 08247. They make their own ice cream (more than 50 flavors) at this old-fashioned parlor, which has been in Stone Harbor since Prohibition. You can eat in, or take your cone, gelato, or sorbet to eat outside on one of the many benches. They'll make custom milk shakes, too. Expect to wait on weekends in summer: The line stretches down the block. No credit cards. Open 11 AM–11 PM in-season. $.

Sylvester's (609-967-7553; sylvesters-avalon.com), 503 21st St., Avalon 08202. Eat your meal under the awnings, or call ahead to take home seafood meals from this popular eatery. Sylvester's also carries pasta dishes, platters, and sandwiches. BYOB. Lunch, dinner in-season. $$.

Tonio's Pizza (609-368-5558), 2475 Ocean Dr., Avalon 08202. Tonio's dishes up more than just pizza, even if that's the most popular item after midnight. The wings are some of the best on the island. For a double dose of Tonio's favorites, go for the Buffalo-chicken-topped pizza. Lunch, dinner, late night. $.

Tortilla Flats (609-967-5658), 2540 Dune Dr., Avalon 08202. The Mexican food is authentic at this casual eatery. Don't skip out on the warm tortilla chips brought to your table, and it's worth ordering a side of freshly made guacamole to go with them. If you're eating on the go, Tortilla Flats has its own take-out kitchen up the street at 26th and Dune Drive, which is also open for lunch. Dinner in-season. $$.

Via Mare (609-368-4494; viamareavalon.com), 2319 Ocean Dr., Avalon 08202. You'll find large portions of pasta and seafood favorites at this upscale restaurant on Ocean Drive. You can't miss with the frutti de mare—it dishes up the best of what the ocean and Via Mare have to offer. Dinner. Closed late Nov.–mid-Feb. $$$.

Windrift (800-453-7438; wwin driftbar.com), 125 80th St., Avalon 08202. You can get just about any kind of food at the Windrift, from fried shore staples in the Dining Room to sushi and oysters in the Signature Lounge. The Windrift is big on nightlife. The Deck is a popular post-beach spot, with lots of people, drinks, and sandy feet. The indoor bar is an Avalon staple, and people come for the atmosphere, the regulars, and the cover bands that play hits reaching back to the '60s. Wing night is on Tuesday in-season. The smaller kitchen in the bar portion of the Windrift will prepare thousands of wings per night. Breakfast, lunch, dinner in-season. $$.

Atlantic Book Shops (609-368-4393; atlanticbooks.us), 261 96th St., 106 Harbor Square Mall, Stone Harbor 08247. This is as close as you'll get to a bookstore chain at the Jersey Shore. Atlantic has locations in just about every town in this book. They stock new titles, bargain books, maps, magazines, and items for the kids. Open 9 AM–10 PM in-season. Call for off-season hours.

Cape May County Park & Zoo (609-465-5271; co.cape-may.nj.us), Rt. 9 & Crest Haven Rd., Cape May Court House 08210. The Cape May County Park & Zoo isn't just a zoo. Its 85 acres also include a park with picnic grounds, playgrounds, woods, a pond, a gazebo, and now a disc-golf course. The zoo has more than 550 animals representing 250 species of mammals, birds, amphibians, and reptiles. Zoo open 10 AM–4:45 PM in-season, 10–3:45 off-season. Park open 9 AM–dusk. Closed Christmas. Free, though you are asked for a donation.

Garden Greenhouse (609-624-1350; gardengreenhouse.net), 1919 Rt. 9 N., Cape May Courthouse 08210. Sure, the Garden Greenhouse does a lot of landscaping work, but anyone who appreciates living things will enjoy a stroll through their garden center. It's a special treat in winter when Christmas gifts are added in, and Santa comes to town. Open 9 AM–5 PM.

Hollywood Bicycle Center (609-967-5500; hollywoodbikeshop.com), 2522 Dune Dr., Avalon 08202. Rent your ride at this bike shop, or look for

Hollywood Bicycle Center   Courtesy of Scott Neumyer

something new. They also repair bikes and offer free air for your tires. Make sure to check out the collection of Simpsons, Pee-wee Herman, and Austin Powers toys that line the shop's ceiling. Open 8:30 AM–5 PM Mon., Tue., Thu., Fri., and Sat.; 10–5 PM Sun.

Leaming's Run Gardens (609-465-5871; leamingsrungardens.com), 1845 Rt. 9 N., Cape May Court House 08210. This private garden—the largest annual garden in the country—features more than 30 acres of ferns, lawns, ponds, and more. Leaming's has over 25 individually designed gardens to explore and enjoy, and plenty of benches are provided throughout. The best time to visit is in August when the hummingbirds come back to town. Open 9:30 AM–5 PM, mid-May–Oct. $.

Lighten Up (800-679-5747; lightenuponline.com), 283 96th St., Stone Harbor 08247. You'll find toys for kids and grown-ups at this whimsical store, which is owned by the father-and-son pair of Todd and Shem Jenkins. They have a big selection of kites, wind socks, flags, toys, mind-bending puzzle games, and juggling equipment, as well as marbles. Make sure you visit the upstairs level—it's a high-flying adventure. Open 10 AM–10 PM in-season, 11–4 off-season.

Mimi's Shop & SunCatcher Surf Shop (609-368-3488; suncatchersurf.com), 9425 2nd Ave., Stone Harbor 08247. Between Mimi's and SunCatcher, you'll find surf gear, surf wear, and upscale styles for the family. You might get a little lost winding from section to section, but they've got everyone from your tweens to your grandfather covered. Expect a lot of surf and skate staple brands, like Billabong, Volcom, O'Neill, and Roxy. The women's items lean more upscale, with Nicole Miller and Vera Bradley among the stock. If you're a bargain shopper, check out the Attic, which is located next door and features Mimi's and SunCatcher clothing at deep discounts. Open 10 AM–10 PM in-season. Call for off-season hours. Attic open in-season only.

Murdough's Christmas Shop

Murdough's Christmas Shop (609-368-1529), 256 96th St., Stone Harbor 08247. It's been Christmas at Murdough's for more than 50 years. Get what you need to trim or tree, or add to your Department 56 Christmas building collection. They also sell advent calendars, Christmas cards, and even Halloween items. Make sure to say hello to the golden retriever who rests behind the counter, and check the DAYS LEFT UNTIL CHRISTMAS board as you leave. Open 10 AM–10 PM in-season. Call for off-season hours.

Paper Peddler (609-967-4542), 2538 Dune Dr., Avalon 08202. Paper Peddler sells books, magazines, and activity books for the family in this slip of a store that's been offering great reads since before you could read the news online. You might even be tempted to pick up a few titles for your post-vacation reading. They can order in books within two to three days if they don't have something that appeals to your taste, or if you need a specific title. Open 7:30 AM–10 PM in-season.

Hoy's vs. Seashore Ace

Hoy's and Seashore Ace are both stores in Stone Harbor that sell everything you could possibly need for your shore vacation. But which is better for suntan lotion? A coffee maker? Souvenirs? Beach chairs? I asked a few shore regulars (e.g. my parents, who between them have over 80 years of shore experience) where they'd go for what you forgot to pack:

Hoy's	**Seashore Ace**
609-368-4697	609-368-3191
219 96th St., Stone Harbor	260 96th St., Stone Harbor
08247	08247
	www.seashoreace.com
Toys	
Puzzles	Cooking utensils
Playing cards	Cooking gadgets
Beach games	Paper and plastic utensils
Books	Beach chairs
Flip flops	Outdoor furniture
Suntan lotion	Beach towels
Hats	Tools
Postcards	Hardware supplies
Snacks	Sports equipment
Cold drinks	
Boogie Boards	

Paw Prints (609-368-3700; pawprintsofstoneharbor.com), 281 96th St., Stone Harbor 08247. Spoil your dog or cat with items from this pet shop. They carry collars and leashes with summer and sports team themes, plus doggy Christmas cards and treats. Make sure to check out the second-floor sale area. Open 9 AM–10 PM in-season. Call for off-season hours.

Pirate Island Golf (609-368-8344; pirateislandgolf.com), 2728 Dune Dr., Avalon 08202. Arrrrr, mateys! Belly up to this pirate-ship mini golf course if you dare. The course has enough hazards and traps that it's challenging to even the most seasoned mini golf pros. Open 9 AM–11:30 PM in-season.

She Be Surfin' (609-967-3110; shebesurfin.com), 2516 Dune Dr., Avalon 08202. Surf-inspired fashions for tweens, teens, and women with a knack for beachy style are sold at this elevated shop. They also offer surf lessons for girls and women that are taught by women. Open 9 AM–10 PM in-season. Call for off-season hours.

Stone Harbor Bird Sanctuary (stone-harbor.nj.us/Bird-Sanctuary/Site/Introduction.html), 11400 3rd Ave., Stone Harbor 08247. These 21 acres have been saved for the birds since 1965, and, as a National Natural Landmark by the National Park Service, won't be falling to condo projects anytime soon. What kinds of birds can you expect to find? American, snowy, and cattle egrets are known to nest here, along with Louisiana, great blue, green, little blue, yellow, and black crowned night herons, plus glossy ibises. Free.

Pirate Island Golf   Courtesy of Scott Neumyer

Teaberry Antiques, Collectibles & Gifts (609-624-1700; teaberryantiquesnj.com), 1944 Rt. 9, Clermont 08210. Browse for hidden treasure among more than 65 indoor kiosks. It's not all antiques, though. Vendors also sell gourmet foods, Christmas decorations (all year), home decor, furniture, and costume jewelry. There's even a vendor who sells old magazine advertisements, ready for framing. Teaberry is attached to Avalon Coffee, so feel free to grab a bite or a drink to sip on while taking a look at what Teaberry has to offer. Open 10 AM–6 PM.

Avalon Boardwalk

The Avalon boardwalk is relatively short, clocking in at just 0.5 mile. It's not a hub of activity, either, except for a few eateries and one video arcade. Bikes are allowed on the boardwalk in-season 5–10 AM.

Wave One Sports (609-368-0050; waveonestoneharbor.com), 225 96th St. #225, Stone Harbor 08247. They don't sell just any old shore gear at Wave One. Their items, which range from embroidered sweatshirts to hats to T-shirts to sweatpants, are high quality and last for years (I have three sweatshirts older than my college diploma). Look out for the sale bin, which is where odds and ends are piled together. The Stone Harbor location is larger than their Cape May outpost and also stocks brand-name sports gear from the likes of Nike and Under Armour: everything from running shoes to soccer-ready shorts to sports bras. Open 9 AM–10 PM in-season. Call for hours off-season.

The Wetlands Institute (609-368-1211; wetlandsinstitute.org), 1075 Stone Harbor Blvd., Stone Harbor 08247. Learn about the ecosystems around you at the Wetlands Institute. It's a water wonderland with hands-on exhibits, a "terrapin station," nature trail, observation decks, and children's area with interactive exhibits. It'll make you think twice about dumping your trash on the shore. In 2010, they welcomed a new member to their family: Octavia the Octopus. She's ready to meet you. Open 9:30 AM–4:30 PM Mon.–Thu. and 10–4 Sun. in-season; open 9:30–4:30 Tue.–Sat. off-season. $.

Wetsuit World (609-368-1500; wetsuitworld.com), 9716 3rd Ave., Stone Harbor 08247. Buy or rent your perfect wet suit, rash guard, or board at Wetsuit World. They've got gear to protect your skin, whether you're surfing, diving, Jet Skiing, wake boarding, or kite surfing. They also have snorkeling equipment, offer surf lessons, and repair surfboards. Open 10 AM–6 PM Mon.–Thu.; 10–8 Fri.–Sat., 10–6 in-season. Open Fri.–Sun. off-season.

48 Hours

DAY 1

Start your day with sticky buns from the Bread & Cheese Cupboard—*and read the directions on page 115*. You think I'm kidding. I'm not. I've tested this out many, many times.

Then make a stop at the Hollywood Bicycle Center to either rent a ride or get your bike checked out. Be sure you look around the store, too.

Frugal Finds

The Attic, 9407 2nd Ave., Stone Harbor 08247. This slip of a shop is next door to Mimi's Shop & SunCatcher Surf Shop, and sells whatever didn't quite move at the main shop. Labor Day weekend, they'll drop the prices to $20 per item, even if it started out as a $300-plus cocktail dress. I always visit around Memorial Day to get the pick of the shop, then stop back on Labor Day weekend to see what $20 options are left. Open in-season. Call for hours.

Barrier Island Trading Post (609-368-1415), 9501 3rd Ave., Stone Harbor 08247. Take a detour to this off-the-main-street used-book store and you're sure to score a bargain. Most books are priced between $1 and $5. They also stock rare first editions and collectible books, as well as select new titles and CDs. You can trade in your books for store credit—but if it's a hardcover you'd like to trade in, it must have the dust jacket. Open 10 AM–10 PM in-season. Call for off-season hours.

Barries Shoes (609-368-8200; barrieshoes.com), 9501 3rd Ave., Stone Harbor 08247. Barries sells comfort shoes, like Naturalizer, Hush Puppy, New Balance, Sperry, and Minnetonka, at outlet prices. They stock narrow and wide sizes, too, plus flip-flops and handbags. Take note: The shoes are *not* irregulars, damaged goods, or so ridiculously out of style that it would be natural to see them priced so low. Open 10 AM–5 PM.

Wave One Sports (609-368-0050; waveonestoneharbor.com), 221 96th St. #225, Stone Harbor 08247. For the real deal, don't go into Wave One Sports. Go into the store across the hallway—it looks like it stocks exclusively Under Armour clothing—and walk to the back. There you'll find closeout items from Wave One and from Avalon's She Be Surfin'. Final sale only, so make sure you love love love it before you buy.

It's worth it. Then, after you pedal around the island—which is a very popular thing to do—bike your way over to the Stone Harbor Bird Sanctuary, which is 100 percent free and a great way to see as many birds as you can in a short period of time without leaving the island.

Hungry yet? Sure you are—you're biking a lot. Stop at Green Cuisine for a filling yet healthy meal. You did, after all, sweet- and carb-load this morning on sticky buns.

Next up: Pirate Island Golf. It's good for kids and adults alike, and challenging for everyone. Tonight, check out the Diving Horse, an upscale BYOB in Avalon that centers its menu on whatever is local and fresh at the time.

Then head across Dune Drive for a drink at the Princeton, aka the P. If you're looking for a long night out with hundreds of your closest friends, park yourself here for the duration. If not, get out by 9 PM and cross over to the Rockin' Chair—or check out the deck at the Windrift for those wonderful sea breezes.

DAY 2

Start day 2 with breakfast at Brian's Waffle House—if you're like me and allergic to eggs, they have plenty of non-omelet options. Then head slightly off the island to the Wetlands Institute, which is a wonderful educational center with a special section where kids can learn all they ever wanted to know about the environment. It's good for grown-ups, too. Ask to go to the observation lookout.

Then keep going over the causeway along Route 9, which is known for its antiques—make sure to hit Teaberry Antiques for a hodgepodge of antiques and collectibles. Wave to Avalon Campground for me. It's where I spent my childhood summers.

Head back to the island for lunch at the Concord Café, which has my favorite bar food on the island. Follow that up with a stroll down 96th Street in Stone Harbor for upscale shopping and souvenirs.

Ready for dinner? Head to the Sea Grill for an upscale meal. Have dessert if

The dunes in Avalon

you like. But your best bet? Back to Stone Harbor for a cone from Springer's. You'll encounter a line, but it's worth the wait. Trust me.

Extend Your Stay

If you have more time, try these great places to see and things to do . . .

Like nature? Head to Leaming's Run Gardens, which is the largest annual garden in the country. Or if you're bringing the kids, check out the Cape May County Zoo, which is free (though they do ask for a donation).

Bargain shoppers must head to the Attic, which has the odds and ends that didn't quite sell in SunCatcher and Mimi's. I scored a Nicole Miller gown for $30 recently. The prices drop as the summer season progresses. Best deals are on Labor Day weekend, when everything's $20 max.

Turtle Power

The shore is busiest in summer, and not just for humans. It's prime time for turtles as well. Summer is when female diamondback terrapins lay their eggs, and their nesting grounds just happen to be near the causeways that bring tourists from the inland areas to the shore.

What can you do? To start, be careful when driving on the causeways, and through Strathmere. The island is narrow enough that turtles try to cross the road.

If you see a turtle on the side of the road, stop and put him or her back into the salt marshes, or call the **Wetlands Institute** in Stone Harbor at 609-368-1211. They work through the nesting season to make sure turtles—and their nests—stay safe.

If you see a turtle that's been killed, that doesn't mean that it's a lost cause. The Wetlands Institute will take recently killed female turtles and harvest their eggs, incubate them, and then hatch the young. If you're willing to bring a killed turtle to the institute, make sure to wrap the body in plenty of towels and plastic. They bleed profusely, but you'll be helping preserve an important part of the wetlands ecosystem. Or call the Wetlands Institute and they'll come out to collect the turtle.

Special Events

Festivals, parties, and happenings down the shore

YEARLY

May

Sail into Summer Weekend (609-886-8600, ext. 17; stoneharbor beach.com), 95th St. Parking Lot, Stone Harbor. Preview the upcoming summer season at this annual festival, which includes boat and seafood shows. The Chowder Fest is worth its weight in clams. $.

June

Avalon Chamber of Commerce Craft Fair (609-967-3936; avalonboro.org). Check out the best of local wares at this annual craft show.

July

Stone Harbor Baby Parade (609-368-6101), 96th St., Stone Harbor. You know your baby's cute—let the world know, too, or check out the other toddling tots. Free.

Tour de Shore (609-967-3456; princetonbar.com). Tour de Shore is part Halloween party, part bike parade, part bar crawl. Register your team, dressed in a theme, at the Princeton and then move en masse from one Avalon bar to another. Make sure you come up with something interesting to do on stage when your team is introduced to the crowd. The money raised is for charity, not just fun. Previous themes have included angels and devils; the Roman legislature; future cougar bait; and 5-year-old's birthday party. It's as interesting as your team makes it. $$.

September

Nun's Beach Community Day and Surf Invitational, 111th St. beach, Stone Harbor. This surf festival is held at Nun's Beach in Stone Harbor, which is right by Villa Maria, a convent of Immaculata IHM. Yes, you could see a nun on a surfboard.

Wings & Water Festival (609-368-1211; wetlandsinstitute.org), Wetlands Institute. Celebrate (and support) the rich wildlife of New Jersey's

The Brendan

In 1991, Brendan Borek lost his battle with Ewing's sarcoma, a rare pediatric bone cancer. He was only 16, and before he passed away, friends organized a surf competition in his honor. Since then, "The Brendan" has been held in his memory, but it's much more than a surf day now. The event is the cornerstone of a project that raises funds to support area families whose children are suffering from cancer. The High Tides Memorial Fund pays for whatever a family needs—gas and tolls to and from hospitals (usually in Philadelphia), hotels, scholarships, groceries, utilities, mortgages, rent. They make gift baskets around the holidays and even give siblings of children with cancer gift certificates for back-to-school shopping.

"I didn't want other families to go through the experiences we went through as a family," Lydia Borek said.

A big chunk of the money that the High Tides Memorial Fund raises is from one week in August, a week that includes a fashion show, art show, skateboarding event, and restaurant days where the revenues from specific menu items go toward the fund. The crowning event is that surf competition that kicks of bright and early at 6:30 AM on Saturday. It's followed by a homecoming party in town. It's a nice cap to a long week that's doing a great thing for local families.

For more information, visit brendansfund.org.

Renting a Shore House

Many Jersey Shore visitors opt to rent a house or condo for their vacation rather than rent a room at a hotel, motel, or B&B. Ann Delaney, with Tim Kerr's Power Play Realty (who runs an excellent blog about the Seven Mile Island at anndelaney.com) offers these four tips:

1. Ask an agent. Search the websites, sure, but remember that nothing compares with talking with a local agent who is familiar the area and its properties. As an agent, I find it helpful to know where the prospective tenant has stayed in the past to understand their "vision" of a shore vacation.

2. Know what your family needs. Do you have special requests? A pet, handicapped family member, allergies? Ask detailed questions to be sure the property is a good fit for your family.

3. Ask what you're getting. Keep in mind that the shore rental properties are all privately owned. No two are alike. Some are better equipped and maintained. Many owners do not provide beach tags. Not all have wireless Internet, although this is becoming more common.

4. Ask what you're not getting. Renting a home requires some work. Tenants bring their own sheets and towels.

coast at this annual event. Kids (and, okay, you) will enjoy the turtle release, touch tank, and retriever dogs in action. Also boat rides, kayaking, a rubber duck race, crafting, jugglers, folk music, salt-marsh safaris, and dune walks. It all benefits the Wetlands Institute. $.

November

Christmas in Stone Harbor (609-368-6101). This isn't just any holiday event. Along with traditional Christmas festivities like tree trimming and crafts, Thanksgiving weekend is a dog celebration in Stone Harbor. There's even a parade where you can dress up like a four-legged friend. Free.

Important Info

Where to turn when you need to know

EMERGENCY NUMBERS

In an emergency, dial 911.
Poison information: 800-222-1222.
Avalon non-emergency police:
609-967-8299.

Stone Harbor non-emergency police: 609-368-2111.

HOSPITALS

96th Street Urgent Care (609-368-3500; 96thstreeturgentcare.com), 376 96th St., Suite 2, Stone Harbor 08247.
Avalon Medical Center (609-967-3800), 2355 Ocean Dr., Avalon 08202.
Cape Regional Medical Center (609-463-2000; caperegional.com), 2 Stone Harbor Blvd., Cape May Courthouse 08210.

The Woodland Village

If you're headed to Garden Greenhouse (or even if you're not), you might want to stop by the Woodland Village, which is a cluster of shops set in a shady, quaint setting. You'll find a lot of variety, from beauty items to toys to clothing. It's a fun stop if you're back on Route 9.

NEWSPAPERS

7 Mile Times (609-967-7707; 7MileTimes.com).

REALTORS

Avalon Real Estate (609-967-3001; avalonrealty.com), 30th & Dune Dr., Avalon 08202.
Diller Fisher (877-967-SOLD and 877-368-SOLD; dfrealtors.com), 3101 Dune Dr., Avalon 08202, and 9614 3rd Ave., Stone Harbor 08247.
Tim Kerr's Power Play Realty (800-682-5940; powerplayrealty.com), 2821 Dune Dr., Avalon 08202.

TRANSPORTATION

C&C Cab Company (609-399-9100), 115 13th St., Ocean City 08226.
Enterprise Rent A Car (609-522-1119; enterprise.com).
Yellow Cab (609-263-2225).

TOURISM CONTACTS

Avalon Chamber of Commerce (609-967-3936; avalonbeach.com).
Stone Harbor Chamber of Commerce (609-368-6101; stoneharborbeach .com).
New Jersey Travel and Tourism (800-VISITNJ; state.nj.us/travel).

5

The Wildwoods

THRILLS AND SPILLS

HISTORY

THE WILDWOODS is not one town. It's four towns that share the same island: North Wildwood, Wildwood, Wildwood Crest, and West Wildwood.

Explorers Henry Hudson and Robert Juet discovered that island in 1609. In the 1870s, the Wildwoods were home to offshore farmers who let their animals graze on the land. The Hereford Inlet Lighthouse was built in 1874; soon after, the Borough of Wildwood was born, incorporated in 1895.

The Wildwoods were sleepy barrier-island shore towns before the 1950s. Only after World War II did Wildwood become a major tourist destination for Philadelphians. They had a little extra money in their pockets and could afford to pack up the family and spend part of their summer down the shore. The Wildwoods also drew an A-list crowd and became the summertime home to the Las Vegas set since air-conditioning hadn't yet cooled down the desert. Chubby Checker first performed the "Twist" at Wildwood's Rainbow Club, and Dick Clark's first national broadcast of *American Bandstand* was from the Starlight Ballroom on the Wildwood boardwalk in 1957. The nightlife boomed, and so did construction, especially of motels, which were then a new concept. You didn't have to walk down long corridors to get to your room; you just drove up and went into your temporary vacation home.

But prosperity and fortunes shifted. The motels started showed their age, Vegas got air-conditioning, and Atlantic City allowed legal gambling. Wildwood didn't swing like it used to, and many of the family-friendly spots disappeared. The Wildwood boardwalk became a place you didn't take your kids anymore because of seedy T-shirt shops and tattoo parlors.

LEFT: Raging Waters   Courtesy of Marc Steiner/Agency New Jersey

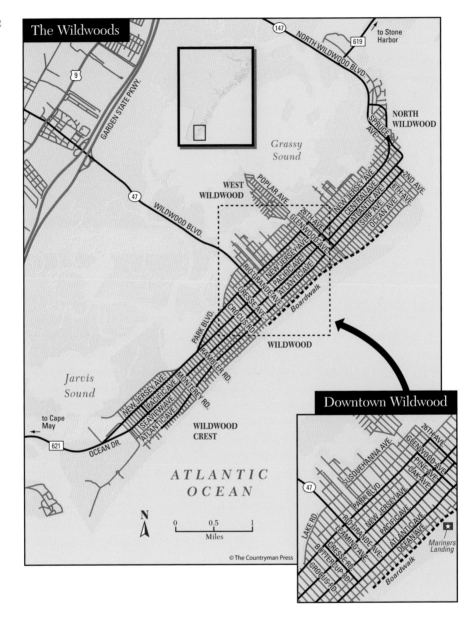

It took a group of concerned citizens to save one of the things that made Wildwood special—Doo Wop architecture—in the form of the Doo Wop Preservation League. Instead of thinking these funky buildings were passé, the town celebrated its kitsch and worked to preserve this unique corner of history. Wildwood has more than 50 of these vintage motels—the largest concentration in the country. Without the Doo Wop Preservation

League, there'd be far fewer. Wildwood had 100 such midcentury buildings until 2000, which is when developers went demolition-crazy and knocked a lot down to put up condos and duplexes in their place. You'll find most of the survivors in Wildwood Crest on a 2-mile stretch between Atlantic and Ocean Avenues.

Today the Wildwoods have what still attracts families to the shore: a 1.85-mile boardwalk, amusement rides, nightclubs, and, of course, the beach. The Wildwoods have long beaches, too—up to 1,000 feet wide in some places—and they're free (most other South Jersey Shore towns require beach tags in-season). The boardwalk is no longer one long strip of seediness, though you'll still find a few of those T-shirt shops and tattoo parlors. It also has rides—lots of them, more than Disney World. And the towns have worked to bring a variety of events to the island that are attracting visitors year-round. The Fabulous '50s and Sensational '60s weekends, Irish Fall Festival, and Roar to the Shore attract tens of thousands of visitors. The construction of a new convention center has given the towns the room and the ability to rebuild their tourism base year-round.

The Wildwoods could be teetering on the edge of another, more troubling change. You'll see a lot of foreclosure signs, evidence that the area was built up too quickly during the housing boom, and fell hard in the bust. Recent changes in liquor laws that allow restaurants on the boardwalk to

Welcome to Wildwood   Courtesy of Marc Steiner/Agency New Jersey

serve beer. It threatens the family-friendly feel tha the Wildwoods have worked so hard to rebuild.

Even though all three towns on the island work together to promote tourism, each has a distinct feel. North Wildwood is more residential and has the widest beaches; the nightlife leans to the cozy, quaint Irish pub scene. Wildwood is what sizzles with the bulk of the boardwalk action (and houses that are rented out by teenagers for prom and senior weeks). Wildwood Crest is home to many of the island's Doo Wop buildings, and has lakefront areas that offer sunset views. West Wildwood is a 0.25-square-mile island that's in a world of its own with one bridge on and off, one bar, and its own fire and police departments.

Wherever you plan to stay, you're close to everything the Wildwoods have to offer—the island, after all, only 5 miles long.

Pick Your Spot

Best places to stay in and around the Wildwoods

Ala Kai Motel (609-522-2159; alakaimotel.com), 8301 Atlantic Ave., Wildwood Crest 08260. Polynesian kitsch rules at this beach-block spot, which is one of the original Doo Wop style motels. The vintage bamboo-lettered neon sign has been refurbished so that the hula girl shines her brightest again. The tiki theme continues in your room, where the beds are adorned in wild, flower-printed bedspreads. Ala Kai has a pool, and you can rent one-room suites, or one- and two-room efficiencies. Open in-season. $$–$$$.

The American Inn (609-729-7700; americaninn.com), 510 E. 13th Ave., North Wildwood 08260. You can't beat the location: right across the street from the beach,

and just steps from the entrance to the Wildwood boardwalk. Rooms are simple but clean. Same for the on-site pool. All rooms come with kitchen and microwave. Open in-season. $$.

The Caribbean (609-522-8292; caribbeanmotel.com), 5600 Ocean Ave., Wildwood Crest 08260. Built in 1957 by Lou Morey, the Caribbean was considered ultra-modern for its time. It featured plastic palm trees, a crescent-shaped pool, and a "Jetson ramp" that curved from the second-story sundeck down to the hotel's lounge. In 2004, George Mill and Carolyn Emigh bought the Caribbean and restored it. The exterior doesn't look all that different from when the place opened, but almost everything inside has changed, from the plumbing to the decor. They're big on events here. If you book a room for a holiday weekend, or for national or local festivals (Kentucky Derby, Fabulous Fifties Weekend,

Savings in the Shoulder Seasons

If you're looking for a deal, get down the shore one of the shoulder seasons of spring or fall. The weather might not be summer heat, but the shore is less crowded and less expensive. If you're not concerned with getting kids back to school, book the week leading up to Labor Day weekend. You'll hit the shore at the tail end of summer, and usually at a discount since so many people take that week to get ready for the school year.

Italian Festival), expect a feast to be part of your stay. All guests are invited to their holiday special meals. Open Apr.–Oct. $$.

Lollipop Motel (609-729-2800; lollipopmotel.com), 2301 Atlantic Ave., Wildwood 08260. You can't miss the Lollipop. The exterior is graced with a giant, 50-year-old lollipop (no, not actually candy) and the faces of two very happy kids. The candy theme continues to the multicolored doors and eye-popping poolside umbrellas, but the rooms are more what you'd find in a modern motel. Open in-season. $$–$$$.

Montego Bay Resort (609-523-1000; montegobayresortnj .com), 1700 Boardwalk, North Wildwood 08260. Hard to miss

Montego Bay: It's bright yellow and right on the boardwalk in North Wildwood. It's also near the finish line for the Ocean Drive 10-Miler, a late-March race that I run every year. Pick one of their suite-style accommodations, or drop by to visit their indoor water park, which includes indoor pool, Jacuzzi, waterslide, kids' area, tiki bar, and flat-screen TVs. $$.

Nova Motel (609-522-3193; dawnmotelnj.com/nova_index.html, 4300 Ocean Ave., Wildwood 08260. The Nova is a classic Wildwood motel close to the Wildwoods Convention Center, and—best of all for us dog lovers—some of their rooms are dog-friendly. Don't expect anything too fancy, but if you want to vacation with Fido in Wildwood, this is a great option. Rooms were renovated in 2009. Open May–Oct. $.

The Starlux (609-522-7412; thestarlux.com), 305 E. Rio Grande Ave., Wildwood 08260. The Starlux started as the Wingate, a typical 1950s Wildwood motel. Rooms back then cost $8–10 a night and offered "Free Drive-In Parking!" The bones of the Wingate are still part of the Starlux, but the building was gutted in 2000 and expanded in 2002 into a 39-room boutique hotel with an Astro Lounge, a pool and hot tub where the parking lot used to be, and two Airstream trailers tricked out, modernized, and available for rent. Guests get free bike rentals and access to that Astro Lounge, which is the setup space

The Starlux   Courtesy of Morey Family Archives

for continental breakfast and has a flat-screen TV, DVDs, and an area to hang out if the weather's not beach-friendly. $–$$$.

Summer Nites (800-ROC-1950; summernites.com), 2110 Atlantic Ave., North Wildwood 08260. Sheila and Rick Brown have turned the B&B concept on its head with Summer Nites. Sure, the building might look like your typical shore home, but the classic car parked outside is a hint about the goodies inside. Elvis and Marilyn are in the building—plus rooms dedicated to '50s television and movies, the '60s, and the '70s, among others. Each room is meticulously decorated, from the custom, hand-painted headboards and murals, to *Grease*-decorated light switches, to the gold lamé couches in the Elvis room. Guests can also play tunes on the jukebox or pick up a bottle of Coke from a vintage, working Coke dispenser (dimes are provided). If you're a big fan of the King, Summer Nites has two Elvis weekends, plus a New Year's Eve party. No children allowed. $$.

"Watch the Tram Car, Please"

(609-523-TRAM; dowildwood.com) Wildwood Boardwalk Sightseer Tram Cars have been taking people up and down the boardwalk since 1949. The recording that blares out of the bright yellow-and-blue cars—"Watch the Tram Car, Please"—was made by Floss Stingel and has been in use since those original cars rumbled up and down the boardwalk.

The cars were created in 1939 for the World's Fair and bought by Gilbert Ramagosa for the Wildwood boardwalk. Eight are in service—five originals from 1939—and give rides to about 500,000 people a year. The trams run continuous loops from Cresse Avenue at the Wildwood/Wildwood Crest border to 16th Street in North Wildwood, and stop at all the hot boardwalk stops. A ride will cost you $2.50 each way. The carts start rolling part-time on Easter weekend and, in-season, 11 AM–1 AM.

In 2007, new tram cars were added to the fleet—the first time in 44 years—and run the same route just as those original cars from 1939 do. The new carts look the same but have better cushioning and better tires. And who cut the ribbon introducing those new cars to the fleet on June 27, 2007? Floss Stingel, of course. And yes, she did give a live rendition of her famous call.

Watch the tramcar, please! Courtesy of The Wildwoods

Local Flavors

Taste of the town—local restaurants, cafés, bars, bistros, etc.

Casey's on Third (609-522-7759), 301 New York Ave., North Wildwood 08260. Relax with some drinks, friends, fun, and maybe a seat at the bar watching sports at this corner bar. They have live bands, too. This is probably the best spot if you're hoping *not* to be run over by the massive crowds that hit North Wildwood every September for the town's Irish Weekend. Lunch, dinner. $.

Claude's (609-522-0400; claudesrestaurant.com), 100 Olde New Jersey Ave., North Wildwood 08260. Oo la la—yes, there is French dining in the Wildwoods, and you'll find it at Claude's. The husband-and-wife chef-owner pair put their culinary know-how into the menu. Claude Pottier takes care of the cuisine, preparing savory items like pork, duck, and lamb, and Mary Pottier handles the desserts, like the triple berry pie. Reservations recommended. Dinner in-season. Closed Tue. $$$.

Doo Wop Diner (609-522-7880; doo-wopdiner.com), 4010 Boardwalk, Wildwood 08260. Get a taste of history and the boardwalk at this diner. The menu isn't stuck in the past, though. You can get wraps as well as burgers at the retro diner counter or booth. Breakfast is popular here, as are the impossibly thick milk shakes. Breakfast, lunch, dinner in-season. $.

Duffer's Restaurant & Ice Cream Parlor (609-729-1817; www.dufferswildwood.com), 5210 Pacific Ave., Wildwood 08260. You'll find big portions at this AAA-rated family-friendly spot that has a train running through it (a small one—it's along the ceiling). It's part restaurant, part old-fashioned ice cream parlor, and part activity center: There's an arcade, mini golf course, and souvenir shop on-site. Breakfast, lunch, dinner in-season. $.

Fitzpatrick's Crest Tavern (609-522-1200; cresttavern.com), 9600 Pacific Ave., Wildwood Crest 08260. Crest Tavern is your typical hometown, good-time bar. Enjoy

Hot Spots

If you're looking for a quick bite to eat, but aren't sure what that bite should be, head to one of the many Hot Spots in Wildwood. Yes, that's capital *H* and *S* because *Hot Spot* is the proper name of several Wildwood eateries.

The original is at 3401 Boardwalk with sequels in Wildwood and North Wildwood. All the Hot Spots dish up filling and, depending on what you order, greasy-but-good foods like burgers, gyros, and sausages.

Tully Nut

What exactly is a Tully Nut? If I knew, I'd tell you, but the recipe's a secret, and has been since Mark Tully spent the winter of 1969 creating this drink. What I do know is that it has five kinds of liquor and is a favorite at **#1 Tavern** (609-522-1775, supertully nut.com; 1st & Atlantic Ave., North Wildwood 08260). This red, slushy drink is a kicker, though, so one Tully Nut is probably enough if you'd like to be able to walk home under your own power.

good crowds in-season and a laid-back, locals-only gathering spot in the off-season. Pub grub here is excellent, and they do take-out. Lunch, dinner. $.

Groff's Restaurant (609-522-5474; groffsrestaurant.com), 423 E. Magnolia Ave., Wildwood 08260. In 1918, Earl M. Groff moved to Wildwood and operated boardwalk games for vacationers. In 1925, he added a hot dog stand and kept expanding until we have Groff's as it is today. It's still family owned. The menu is classic American with influences from Groff's native Pennsylvania Dutch. Don't skip on the pies. Groff's now sells them for the holidays if you're craving a bit of Wildwood with your turkey and ham. Dinner in-season, weekends only in May and June. Call for pies in Nov. and Dec. $$.

Keenan's Irish Pub (609-729-3344; keenansirishpub.com), 113 Olde New Jersey Ave., North Wildwood 08260. Yes, they serve food at Keenan's, though it's better known as a haven for cover bands and drink specials. The place rocks during the season. They've long held a Memorial Day opening party, starting bright and early the Friday of the long weekend. Lunch, dinner in-season. $.

Marie Nicole's (609-522-5425; marienicoles.com), 9510 Pacific Ave., Wildwood Crest 08260. You'll find elegant dining in a casual setting at Marie Nicole's. You can't go wrong with the wasabi- and sesame-crusted ahi tuna, or the pan-seared salmon—or anything on the menu, really. Check out the knockout wine list. You can eat inside or on the patio. Dinner, late night. $$$$.

Marvis Diner (609-522-0550), 4900 Pacific Ave., Wildwood 08260. In 1965, two sisters from Saratoga opened a diner in Wildwood. They got the business going, then moved on to other projects. They also got married, and each had a son. Those sons brought the Marvis Diner back into the family (the name *Marvis* is a combination of their mothers' names). Today it's a Doo Wop '50s diner with plenty of shiny chrome and bright booths. The food is mostly diner food with dashes of modernity thrown in. Breakfast, lunch, dinner in-season. Call for off-season hours. $.

My Wildwoods

By Amy Z. Quinn

If a resort city's streets could talk, you'd hear Wildwood's sassy mouth a mile away.

If you're about to get in a bar fight, North Wildwood is the chick you want at your back, because she *always* brings friends. West Wildwood's the quiet type, not so much ignored as she is happy to be left alone.

In fact, if we're imagining the Wildwoods as a quartet of sisters, the Crest is the one who left Senior Week behind and settled down with a family. But every now and again, even a grown-up lady likes to party.

For me, it's impossible to think of that clutch of towns along the 5-mile island near New Jersey's southern tip as anything but members of a family, with similar features—the broad, ever-growing beaches connected by that great spine of a boardwalk—yet each a somehow distinct, unique version of the other. It's a collection of flirts and matriarchs, of immigrants and visionaries, living in a world of both grit and luxury.

And always, of possibility.

In the early 1970s, my parents, an industrious blue-collar couple from Philly, saw possibility in a rambling, Depression-era Dutch Colonial up the block from the Firehouse Tavern on Pine Avenue. Behind this big house, ringing a cement courtyard, stood three small cottages, which my parents—their creativity tapped out after selecting names for their six children—dubbed A, B, and C.

For nearly 30 years, they rented the cottages to a rotating cast of characters, usually young people, some looking for a vacation place and others who stayed the summer, working on the boardwalk spinning prize wheels or twisting custard cones. My older sisters, already teenagers in the '70s and '80s, each took their turn living and working in Wildwood, tasting independence for the first time even as my dad hovered protectively nearby.

For part of each year, my mother would install herself in the Big House, her cooking sending the smell of spaghetti sauce wafting through the wrought-iron air vents. She'd spend her days sprucing up the cottages or shopping along Pacific Avenue, leaving my brother and me just enough freedom to roam the neighborhood, which forever smelled of burnt toast owing to the bakery a few blocks away.

In the evenings we'd all sit on the front porch, bodies sunken into aged red-painted wicker rockers, beholding a predictable yet ever-changing parade of people making their way along Pine Avenue toward the beach and boardwalk.

As dusk fell, it would be parents pushing strollers or holding the hands of little ones impatient for that moment when the Tilt-A-Whirl makes its first furious spin. Next would come teenagers, hair-sprayed girls dressed to impress the boys in gold chains who'd have to be home by curfew. Still later, the strollers came back bearing toddlers overtired and cranky or already sound asleep, and young adults would head out for the night, bound for Kelly's Cafe or the Stardust or the old Penalty Box, where the bartenders wore striped shirts and whistles like NHL linesmen.

Of course, everyone knows the island's more recent story, how through a mixture of poor planning, mismanagement, and changing tastes, the good times waned in the Wildwoods. Like an aging party girl, things along the boardwalk became less fun and more tawdry, and Pacific Avenue's charms fell away like flakes of sunburned skin.

These days, I'm happy to say, the things are coming around again in the Wildwoods. Simple economics have led many people back to the island, though of course keeping them there is always the trick.

It surely sounds overly simplistic to say things just *feel* good again in Wildwood, but there it is. I catch the expectant, excited look on my son's face each time we cross that bridge into town and the giant Ferris wheel comes into view, and I know. I see the young couples touring condos for sale, and families pouring out of minivans into neon-lit hotels, and I feel it.

Like I said, possibility.

Amy Z. Quinn is a Philadelphia-area freelance journalist who understands the importance of watching the tram car, please. Read more of her work at citizenmom.net.

Owen's Pub (609-729-7290; owenspub.com), 119 E. 17th St., North Wildwood 08260. Good food, good drinks, and good music—what else could you ask for at a local pub? The dining room is set aside from the bar area, though you'll find flat-screen TVs in both.

The best night to go (and more difficult night to get a seat) is during the weekly "Name That Tune" competition. Lunch, dinner. $.

Pete's Pork Roll (609-552-4411), 3806 Boardwalk, Wildwood 08260. Taylor Pork Roll—known in South Jersey simply as pork roll—is

West Wildwood

If you've never head of West Wildwood, you're not the only one. I surveyed more than a few shore regulars, who all replied with something along the lines of "West where?"

West Wildwood is located over a bridge on 26th Street from Wildwood. It's the only road on and off the island. It is its own borough with its own fire department, police department, mayor, and everything else a township needs, though it doesn't have any traffic signals. No need—it's that small.

It's mostly residential, with year-round or vacationing residents. The bar in town, **Westside Saloon** (609-729-1488; 770 W. Glenwood Ave., West Wildwood 08260), is the kind of place where everyone knows your name, and if they don't, they'll probably ask. West Wildwood is prone to flooding, which is why most of the houses look like they've been lifted up on cinder blocks. Some started on the ground but were raised. Residents take the flooding in stride—one pointed out two areas of higher ground to me where people park their cars until the water levels drop back down.

You won't find much in West Wildwood in terms of nightlife or action, which is why most people like it. It's close to the water and has the same benefits of the shore, but without a lot of traffic—of either the car or the people variety—or noise.

Learn more at westwildwoodnj.com.

one of those foods you must eat when visiting the Jersey Shore, and there's no better place to sample a taste than at Pete's Pork Roll. If ham isn't your thing, they also serve sandwiches, burgers, hot dogs, ice cream, and coffee. Open in-season, weekends only in Oct. $.

Sam's Pizza Palace (609-522-6017; samspizzawildwood.com), 2600 Boardwalk, Wildwood 08260. A Wildwood tradition since 1957. Sam Spera moved to the United States from Italy in 1951 and ran a lunch truck in Trenton. When he

drove with a friend to Wildwood in the summer of 1957, he never left. The thing to get here—obviously—is pizza, but they also serve cheese steaks and pizza steaks. They put an updated menu—in the form of a picture of their price board—on the boardwalk every year. Lunch, dinner. $.

Schellenger's (609-522-0433), 3510 Atlantic Ave., Wildwood 08260. The roof of Schellenger's will catch your eye first—it's packed with sea scenes, like tugboats and a giant lobster hanging over the entrance. The menu is huge and updated often, so ask your server what the latest and greatest may be. Or go with the tried and true, like the lobster bake, which mixes a whole lobster, clams, shrimp, crab, corn on the cob, and potatoes. Dinner in-season; seating starts at 3 PM. $$.

Shamrock Café (609-522-7552), 3700 Pacific Ave., Wildwood 08260. It's straight bar food here,

because what keeps people at the Shamrock late into the night are the drink specials, live music, and the crowds. They have outdoor seating and pool tables, too. Dinner, late night. Lunch Sat.–Sun. $.

Star Diner Café (609-729-4900; wstardinercafe.com), 325 W. Spruce Ave., North Wildwood 08260. The Star Diner has been serving up big portions of hearty diner foods for 40 years, right on

Schellenger's

the way in and out of North Wildwood from the Garden State Parkway. And we're not talking just burgers and fries but full-sized dinner meals. The waffles are an excellent breakfast treat. It's right on your way on and off the island via Route 147, which makes it ideal for saying hello or good-bye to the Wildwoods. On-site bakery. BYOB. Breakfast, lunch, dinner. $.

Westy's Irish Pub (609-522-4991; westysirishpub.com), 101 E. Walnut Ave., North Wildwood 08260. It might be an Irish pub, but they do wings right at Westy's. If you're into a less messy meal, try The Westy; chicken, roasted peppers, Jack cheese, and honey mustard on a baguette. This is a popular late-night spot, too, with live entertainment year-round, plus Quizzo and wing nights. Breakfast, lunch, dinner. $.

Don't Miss This

Check out these great attractions and activities . . .

3J's Wildwood Bowl & Sports Bar (609-729-0111; 3jwildwoodbowl .com), 3401 New Jersey Ave., Wildwood 08260. For over 30 years, 3Js has been setting 'em up for you to knock down—and keeping kids occupied on rainy beach days. If bowling's not your thing, 3J's also has pool tables and Nintendo Wii sports on a big screen. Open 2 PM–midnight Mon., 3–11 Tue., 3–midnight Thu.–Fri., 10 AM–midnight Sat., and noon–10 Sun. $$.

Wildwood   Emil R. Salvini, *Tales of the New Jersey Shore* (Guilford, CT: Globe Pequot Press)

Doo Wop Experience Courtesy of The Wildwoods

Captain Schumann's Whale and Dolphin Watching (800-246-9425), 4500 Park Blvd., Wildwood 08260. Check out the dolphins and whales that travel through New Jersey waters with Captain Schumann, who looks slightly like Santa Claus. He offers three half-hour whale- and dolphin-watching cruises a day in-season. Dogs are welcome aboard—Schumann swears that they can tell what they're looking at. Just call ahead to make sure there's space on the boat for your pet. Open in-season. $$$.

Doo Wop Experience Museum (doowopusa.org/museum/index.html), Ocean Ave., between Burk & Montgomery Aves., Wildwood 08260. Check out the best of Doo Wop style in this 1960s diner converted into an "experience"—it's more than a museum. You'll see samples of the Doo Wop architecture and elements that put Wildwood in the map in the 1950s. If you swing by after dark, you can't miss the neon garden. The Doo Wop Preservation league saved as many of these classic signs as they could when old Doo Wop buildings were torn down. Make sure you check out "The Giant Postcard Exhibition," which recently moved here from the Wildwood Historical Museum. We've run a sample of what you can find on page 151 of this book. It's a sight to see at night. Free.

Games of chance on the Wildwood boardwalk   Courtesy of Marc Steiner/Agency New Jersey

Douglas Fudge (609-522-3875), 3300 Boardwalk, Wildwood 08260. They've been dishing up fudge at Douglas since 1919, and stepping inside their Wildwood location is like taking a step back in time. The walls are still wood-paneled, and the floor is patterned with the Douglas logo. Scottie dogs are all around (it's the company mascot), and they even have a resting area if you'd like to take a break while enjoying your sweet treat. Open 9 AM–10:30 PM in-season. Call for off-season hours.

Gateway 26 Casino (609-523-2600), 26th & Boardwalk, Wildwood 08260. If games of chance are your thing, this is where you want to go. You won't play for cash, but for tickets that you can turn in for prizes like small toys and games, or bigger items including iPods and baseball jerseys. They also have arcade games and those machines where you can try to maneuver the crane to grab a prize. It's a nice place to chill in the air-conditioning on hot summer days. It's open year-round to warm up in winter, too: 9 AM–1 or 2 AM, depending on crowds in-season. $.

Holly Beach Train Depot (609-522-2379; hollybeachtraindepot.com), 4712 Pacific Ave., Wildwood 08260. All aboard! The Holly Beach Train Depot stocks anything a model-train enthusiast could ever want (plus plenty of conductor caps if that's your thing). The shop is named after the real Holly Beach Train Depot, which is what the section of the Wildwoods that is now known as Wildwood was called before the borough incorporated itself. The depot was located one block from where the store now stands. They buy trains, too. Open 10 AM–4 PM Mon.–Sat.

Morey's Piers & Raging Waters (609-522-3900; moreyspiers.com), 3501 Boardwalk, Wildwood 08260. The Wildwood boardwalk has more rides than Disney World, thanks largely to the Morey family. They operate four different ride piers on the boardwalk—three of them the non-water-park variety: Surfside Pier, Mariner's Landing, and Adventure Pier. Each one has thrills and spills for the family. If your idea of fun is screaming while your stomach flips somersaults, this is the place to go. Between the AtmosFEAR!, Great White, Screamin' Swing, Sea Serpent, and Great NorEaster, you'll get more than your fill of the scary stuff. Just hold off on concessions until after you're through—for the good of yourself and of the guests below the rides you'll be enjoying. Yes, they have rides for younger kids, too. You can buy tickets for rides, or wristbands that work in all three parks. For water thrills and spills, check out Raging Waters: a 1,000-foot endless river, complete with shotgun falls, tube rides, and slipper spills. If you're going to be doing the water park, too, you can combine them with ride packages. Hours vary per pier per month. Check the website for details. $.

Sand Jamm (609-522-4650), 2701 Boardwalk, Wildwood 08260. Get your surf gear at this boardwalk shop, which stocks surf-inspired wear as well. If your board is of the wheeled variety, check out the upstairs Skate Shop. Open 10 AM–midnight in-season.

Boardwalk Chapel

(609-522-2307; chapelopc.org), 4312 Boardwalk, Wildwood 08260. In 1945, the Reverend Leslie Dunn opened a chapel right on the boardwalk. Ever since, assistants and volunteers have been picking up where Dunn left off, preaching the ministry of Orthodox Presbyterian Churches of New Jersey. They hold services at 8 PM Mon.–Sat. and 7 on Sun.

Boardwalk Chapel   Courtesy of Mark W. Chesner

For a schedule of what church is hosting services, check the website. In-season only.

Boardwalk Ghost Ship

I got the call early on a Saturday morning in March. "Jack Morey said okay."

This from Terry O'Brien, whom I'd met years before while he was schlepping his karaoke equipment throughout Cape May for what became locally famous "Terry'Oke" nights. A round guy who gloats that he wears a fanny pack to hold his wallet, cigarettes, and keys, Terry had recently given up the full-time karaoke game to work on something for Jack Morey.

The project was shrouded in mystery; all I knew was that it was something going up on the boardwalk that may or may not involve a ship. I'd poked and prodded Terry to give up information, and he wouldn't. Apparently he relayed my interest to Jack Morey, who with his brother runs the Morey organization. Jack's not a mean guy. He's short and compact, like a powder keg. I spent hours in his office listening to him ramble about how much he loves Wildwood and what the city needs to launch itself into the future (I was writing a story about how he had to tear down the Golden Nugget, a beloved Wildwood ride, in order to possibly build a pier-to-pier roller coaster).

Still, I thought I'd get in trouble as I crossed over the boardwalk to meet Terry on that unseasonably warm day. "Hi Jen!" Jack waved at me from a hulk of plywood that was just starting to look like a ship. "Come aboard!"

After I agreed to sign a confidentiality agreement, Jack and Terry walked me through what is now *Ignis Fatuus*—known more commonly as "Ghost Ship."

The concept of *Ignis Fatuus* grew out of an alleged experiment con- ducted on the USS *Eldridge*, a destroyer escort, in Philadelphia in October 1943. Legend has it that the navy used this ship to test Ein- stein's unified field theory, which stated that creating a unified field of electromagnetism around warships would make them invisible.

Apparently, so the conspiracy theorists say, the experiment didn't go according to plan. The ship became invisible, but it also disap- peared, transporting from Philadelphia to Norfolk, Virginia, and back again. In the process some of the sailors on the ship disappeared, some went insane, and others were fused to the ship's hull.

The navy denies everything about this story, but the mystery was enough for Morey to use it as the base of a creepy ghost-ship experi- ence. He created a plot line in which the USS *Eldridge* has been trans- ported to Wildwood, and another ship—*Ignis Fatuus*—is sent out to sea to destroy it. Before the *Eldridge* can be destroyed, the unified field engine acts up again and fuses together the two ships, creating a ghost ship on the Wildwood boardwalk, complete with lost souls roaming the vessel to scare the bejesus out of anyone who dares walk in their midst.

This isn't a sit-down ride. It's a two-story walk-through experience that Terry calls "low gore, high scare." Instead of using blood and guts for frights, they're using animatronics and live actors done up in zombie makeup.

It was little more than plywood and paint when I visited. I hardly recognize the thing now, all black with the undead walking around. It's not for little kids, but it could be a good scare for the older ones—and for you.

Silen's Shoes and Resortwear (609-522-2155), 5000 Pacific Ave., Wildwood 08260. Dress your feet in style at Silen's. They sell Uggs for the family, plus other foot-comfort favorites, like New Balance, Crocs, Tevas, and Clarks. Don't forget the clothes—they stock workout gear as well as T-shirts that declare where you went on vacation. The shoe clearance rack is impressive, though it might take some work to find your size. Open 9 AM–8 PM in-season; 10–3 off-season.

Splash Zone Water Park (609-729-5600; splashzonewaterpark.com), 3500 Boardwalk, Wildwood 08260. Looking for an alternative to the ocean to cool down? Check out Splash Zone Water Park, which has enough speed slides, body flumes, and chutes to tire out the entire family, plus a shaded wading pool for the little ones. They've also got the biggest raft ride on the East Coast, and a 1,000-gallon bucket of water that rains down on the crowd. In-season. $$.

Whaling Wall by Wyland (wylandfoundation.org), Boardwalk Mall, 3800 Boardwalk, Wildwood 08260. The man simply known as Wyland painted nearly 100 wall murals of marine life, including migrating gray whales, breaching humpbacks, and blue whales. The goal was to raise awareness of the life that lives in the ocean. One of these murals is located in Wildwood. This one is of humpback whales, and since it's life-size, it stands 220 feet long and 30 feet high. Free.

Wildwood Harley-Davidson (609-522-7151), 127 W. Rio Grande Ave., Wildwood 08260. This Harley-Davidson outpost has everything a biker could dream of. They rent bikes, too, if you're looking for a sweet ride on your Wildwood vacation, and they have a service shop. Store open 9 AM–6 PM Mon.–Fri., 9–5 Sat., and 10–4 Sun. in-season. Call for off-season hours.

48 Hours

DAY
1

Start your day with a breakfast sandwich from Pete's Pork Roll. You can go with the local favorite, pork roll (also known as Taylor Ham if you're from northern New Jersey), or an egg sandwich. Then hop on your bike, or rent one, for a ride up the Wildwood boardwalk.

The thing to do in Wildwood is lie on the beach, of course, and it'll take you some time to walk down the wide sand to the water. But if it's raining, check out 3J's Wildwood Bowl & Sports Bar for some bowling fun.

Lunch is also on the boardwalk: pizza from Sam's Pizza Palace—just ask for "a slice." They'll know exactly what you're talking about. Then head over to Splash Zone Water Park for an afternoon of slipping and sliding through and down the chutes and slides.

If you're looking for gourmet for dinner, head to Claude's for French fare. Ready for more rides? Of course you are, and Morey's Piers are the place to go. It's largely because of the Moreys that Wildwood has more rides than Disney World.

For a nightcap, head to Keenan's if you're looking for crowds; Owen's if you want a more laid-back nighttime experience.

Beach in Wildwood Courtesy of The Wildwoods

Morey's Pier circa 1983   Copyright © 1983, 2011 (remastered) Douglas Hunsberger

DAY 2

Start day 2 with breakfast at the Marvis diner, which will have something for everyone. Then it's off for a Captain Schumann's Whale and Dolphin Watching tour. He allows dogs aboard—just make sure to call ahead and ask if there's room.

For lunch, grab a bite to eat at the Doo Wop Diner, which is on the boardwalk, then stroll over to Douglas Fudge for, well, fudge of course, but also almost any candy confection you could ask for.

Dinner tonight's at Duffer's Restaurant & Ice Cream Parlor if you're bringing the kids along. It's a restaurant designed with them in mind. If you're looking for more grown-up fare, hit up Fitzpatrick's Crest Tavern. It's where the locals go in Wildwood Crest.

Post-dinner, head to the Doo Wop Experience, which isn't so much a museum as an homage to the architecture that makes Wildwood unique. At night they light up their "neon garden," which is the final resting spot for neon signs that once graced Wildwood motels and restaurants that have since been torn down.

You can't end your vacation without walking the boardwalk at night. The people-watching is some of the best at the Jersey Shore. If you're feeling tired—or even if you're not—hop on the Tram Car. It's tradition.

Extend Your Stay

If you have more time, try these great places to see and things to do . . .

If you can swing it, book your Wildwood stay during one of their festival weekends, because no one does special events like the Wildwoods. Fabulous '50s, Sensational '60s, and the Irish Fall Festival bring thousands to town, even though it's not yet or just past summer.

Special Events

Festivals, parties, and happenings down the shore

WEEKLY (IN-SEASON)

Monday

Captain Ocean's Ecological Program (609-522-2919). Learn more about the ecology of the Jersey Shore at this weekly morning event. Free.

Crest Pier Free Concerts (609-523-0202). This summertime concert series is laid-back and casual—bring your own chair, borrow theirs, or forget chairs all together and dance the night away. Free.

Irish Pipe and Drum Parade (609-523-1602; dowildwood.com). Drink the luck o' the Irish at this weekly event, which runs late June–late Aug., 7:30–9 PM. Free.

Wednesday

String Band Performances (609-523-1602; dowildwood.com). See the string bands strut their stuff along the Wildwood boardwalk. Free.

Thursday

Boardwalk Family Fun Night (609-523-1602; dowildwood.com). Check out parading clowns, characters, and music on these special summer Thursday-night events. Free.

Friday

Fireworks on the Beach (609-523-1602; dowildwood.com). It doesn't need to be the Fourth of July for fireworks to grace the Wildwood sky. Catch the show at 10:30 PM. Free.

YEARLY

March

St. Patrick's Day Celebration and Parade (609-522-7722). Enjoy the best that Ireland has to offer at this annual parade. Noon. Free.

Doo Wop Duathlon (609-374-6495; delmosports.com). Nope, not a triathlon—this race involves a 2-mile run and 12-mile bike ride and ends with a big breakfast for everyone who ran and rode. 8 AM. $$$$.

Sensational '60s Weekend (888-729-0033; fabfifties.com). This three-day event features dance parties, concerts, contests, and a street fair, all in the name of '60s music. Concerts at the Wildwoods Convention Center sell out quick, so book as soon as you know you're ready to rock out.

May

Boardwalk Craft Show (609-522-0378), boardwalk south of the Wildwoods Convention Center. Check out the handmade crafts on display at this week-end festival, 9 AM–5 PM. Free.

Wildwoods International Kite Festival (609-729-9000; wildwoodsnj .com), Wildwoods Convention Center. They're flying high in the sky at this event, which is the largest kite festival in the United States. Inside the Wildwoods Convention Center, you'll find kite builders, competitions, kite-making workshops, and kids' activities. Outside, of course, you'll find kites flying high in the sky. Make sure to catch the Friday-night illuminated night kite fly, which starts at 9. Free.

June

Spring Thunder in the Sand Pro/Am Motocross Races (609-523-8051; thun dermoto.com). Roar on the shore at this early-June event where Wildwood plays host to AMA-sanctioned Pro-Am races for beginners and pros. Free.

Mummers Brigade Weekend (609-729-9000). If you don't know what a mummer is, you might be puzzled by these string bands dressed in detailed and sparkling costumes walking down the street. But it's a Philadelphia tradition that has found a springtime home down the shore. Free.

National Marbles Tournament (304-337-2764; nationalmarblestourna ment.org). For more than 80 years, kids have been coming to Ringer Stadi-um for this national competition, which pits the best mibsters (aka marble shooters) from around the country against one another. Free.

North Wildwood Original Italian-American Festival (609-729-4533; kofc2572.org). Celebrate your Italian roots (or how much you love Italian food) at this annual three-day event.

July

Co-Ed Beach Ultimate Beach Frisbee Tournament (856-696-9705; wild woodultimate.com). It's not just a lazy summer game—Frisbee is serious business, especially at this annual Ultimate Frisbee tournament, which is on the beach. Free.

Summer in Wildwood Courtesy of Mark W. Chesner

Mid-Summer Festival (609-522-5176), Wildwood Crest. Celebrate the height of the summer season at this two-day event, which showcases crafters, music, and food, and includes kids' activities as well. Free.

NJ State BBQ and Blues (njbbq.com; angleseablues.com). Whether you like either or both, this annual festival brings the best from around the state to Wildwood. The BBQ part is the New Jersey State Barbecue Championship, which pits the best of the best from the entire state against one another—for your stomach's delight. The blues part is the Anglesea Blues Festival, which brings regional and national acts to Wildwood to set the right mood for your culinary feast. Many acts play in the local clubs and bars after fair hours as well. Free.

Wildwood Information Center

(609-522-1407), Boardwalk & Schellenger Ave., Wildwood 08260. I'd like to think that if you have this book, you're not scouring the boardwalk for information about where to go, what to do, and where to eat in Wildwood. But! You must stop in for the coupon books that Wildwood vendors put together every year, so you can save money all those fun things to do and places to eat. You can also pick up discount tram car tickets if you know you're going to ride more than a few times. Buying in bulk can save you 10 to 20 percent. Open Sun.–Thu. 9 AM–9 PM, Fri.–Sat. till 10 in-season. Weekends only off-season.

Morey's Piers Beach Lacrosse Tournament (609-522-3900; moreys piers.com). New in 2010, this is one of the only beach lacrosse tournaments in the world. Check out the action on the beach at Schellenger Avenue.

August

Wildwoods Baby Parade (609-729-4000). This has been a Wildwoods tradition since 1909. If you want to enter your kid, register at the Wildwoods Convention Center. The parade starts there and runs to 16th Street in North Wildwood.

United Way of Cape May County Rubber Ducky Regatta (609-729-2002; uwcmc.org/ducky), Raging Waters Water Park. It's quite a sight—more than 10,000 rubber ducks race toward the finish line of the Endless River ride at Raging Waters to raise money for charity. Free.

September

Boardwalk Classic Car Show (609-523-8051; thundermoto.com), Wildwoods Convention Center. Check out the best of rides gone by at this annual event, which is held on the boardwalk and inside the Wildwoods Convention Center. Free.

Irish Fall Festival (800-IRISH-91), North Wildwood. This four-day event celebrates the best of Irish culture and includes dancing, music, food, and crafts. The Wildwoods are heavy with Irish pubs—expect them to be packed, and offering specials. Free.

Mummers String Band Weekend & Strutters Contest (609-522-7722). If you don't know what a mummer is, you might be puzzled by these string bands dressed in detailed and sparkling costumes walking down the street. But it's a Philadelphia tradition that has found a springtime home at the shore. Enjoy their music at this annual parade. This is a weekend-long event and includes strutting contests, a concert, and a string band parade. The events are held at different locations through Wildwood. Free.

Roar to the Shore (609-729-8870; roartotheshoreonline.com). Bring your motorcycle to this annual rally, which draws more than 100,000 bikes (and bikers). Activities include a Biker Bash, pig roast, and Biker Babe competition. Free.

October

Fabulous '50s Weekend (888-729-0033; fabfifties.com), 4501 Boardwalk, Wildwood 08260. This annual event celebrates the Wildwoods' place in music history. Expect dance parties, concerts, a street fair, and contests. The concerts sell out quickly, so get your tickets as soon as you can. Free, except concerts.

December

Family Holiday Celebration (609-729-9000; wildwoodholiday.com), Wildwoods Convention Center. Ring in the holiday season in style at this holiday kickoff weekend, which includes a tree lighting and parade.

Family Holiday Celebration   Courtesy of The Wildwoods

Important Info

Where to turn when you need to know

EMERGENCY NUMBERS

In an emergency, dial 911.
Poison information: 800-222-1222.
North Wildwood, non-emergency police: 609-522-2411.
Wildwood, non-emergency police: 609-522-0222.
Wildwood Crest, non-emergency police: 609-522-2456.

HOSPITALS

Cape Regional Medical Center (609-463-2000; caperegional.com), 2 Stone Harbor Blvd., Cape May Courthouse 08260.

NEWSPAPERS

Wildwood Leader (609-624-8900; thewildwoodleader.com).

TRANSPORTATION

Caribbean Cab Company (609-523-8000).
Checker Cab Company (609-522-1431).
Hertz Rent-a-Car (609-522-0049; hertz.com).
New Jersey Transit (800-582-5946; njtransit.com).
Yellow Cab Company (609-522-0555).

TOURISM CONTACTS

Greater Wildwood Chamber of Commerce (609-729-4000; wildwoods .com).
Greater Wildwoods Tourism Improvement and Development Authority (800-WW-BY-SEA; wildwoodsnj.com).
New Jersey Travel and Tourism (800-VISITNJ; state.nj.us/travel).

6

Cape May

VICTORIAN ENCHANTMENT

HISTORY

CAPE MAY IS, in a word, beautiful. The "Queen of the Seaside Resorts" at the tip of New Jersey is both a year-round community and tourist draw—a quiet, romantic step back in time. It's more than 400 years old and, in its entirety, a National Historic Landmark.

Cape May plays up its Victorian history, even if the town's past stretches back before then. In 1878, a fire wiped out 30 blocks of the town, and what sprang up in the

Congress Street East from Lafayette circa 1905   Courtesy of Emil Salvini, *Summer City by the Sea, An Illustrated History of Cape May, NJ* (Rutgers University Press)

wake of that fire is what you'll see around town today: expansive Victorian buildings—once vacation homes for the wealthiest Philadelphians—that are now charming bed & breakfasts where the innkeeper always knows your name.

That isn't to say Cape May doesn't bustle. Its nightlife is among the most exciting down the shore, but it's not a place where you'll find bars that pack in hundreds of 20- and 30-somethings. The scene is more elegant and sophisticated yet with a casual feel.

Cape May is a romantic spot, too. It's one of the largest destination wedding locations in the United States. That romantic appeal stretches year-round and makes Cape May a destination when most shore towns have

LEFT: The Chalfonte

159

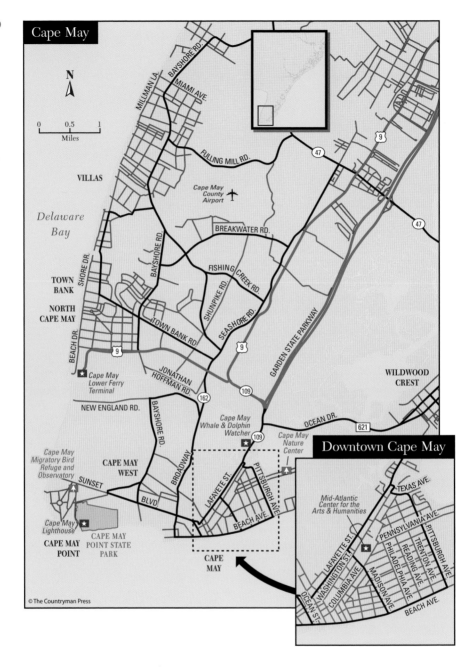

Cape May

N

0   0.5   1
Miles

VILLAS

Delaware Bay

TOWN BANK

NORTH CAPE MAY

MILLMAN LA.

BAYSHORE RD.

MIAMI AVE.

FULLING MILL RD.

Cape May County Airport

BREAKWATER RD.

FISHING CREEK RD.

SHUNPIKE RD.

SEASHORE RD.

BAYSHORE RD.

SHORE DR.

BEACH DR.

TOWN BANK RD.

9

9

47

47

9

GARDEN STATE PARKWAY

WILDWOOD CREST

Cape May Lower Ferry Terminal

JONATHAN HOFFMAN RD.

NEW ENGLAND RD.

162

109

Cape May Whale & Dolphin Watcher

109

Cape May Nature Center

OCEAN DR.

621

Cape May Migratory Bird Refuge and Observatory

CAPE MAY WEST

SUNSET BLVD.

BROADWAY

LAFAYETTE ST.

PITTSBURGH AVE.

BEACH AVE.

Cape May Lighthouse

CAPE MAY POINT

CAPE MAY POINT STATE PARK

CAPE MAY

© The Countryman Press

Downtown Cape May

Mid-Atlantic Center for the Arts & Humanities

TEXAS AVE.

PENNSYLVANIA AVE.

TRENTON AVE.

PITTSBURGH AVE.

PHILADELPHIA AVE.

READING AVE.

LAFAYETTE ST.

WASHINGTON ST.

COLUMBIA AVE.

MADISON AVE.

OCEAN ST.

BEACH AVE.

shut down for the year. While summer is the busiest season—and kids are more than welcome—Cape May is also packed in spring and especially in fall when couples looking to get away turn to the quaint streets, romantic inns, and gourmet restaurants.

The author at Sunset Beach Courtesy of Marc Steiner/Agency New Jersey

Cape May is in a unique geographic position. It's the southernmost point of New Jersey, and because it's here that the Atlantic Ocean meets Delaware Bay, Cape May is home to rich ecosystems. It's along the Atlantic Flyway and a popular resting spot for migratory birds. Don't be surprised to see a lot of people wandering the streets with binoculars around their necks in spring and fall. You can also watch a sunset over the ocean at Sunset Beach at Cape May Point—not an easy thing to do on the East Coast.

Most of Cape May's dining, shopping, and places to stay are in the heart of the city, what's known as Cape May proper. West Cape May and North Cape May are more residential but offer their own delights.

Pick Your Spot

Best places to stay in and around Cape May

Angel of the Sea (800-848-3369; angelofthesea.com), 5 Trenton Ave., Cape May 08204. The two buildings that make up the Angel of the Sea used to be one house. The home was built in 1850 as a summer residence for Philadelphia chemist William Weightman Sr. After construction, Weightman decided that he'd rather have an ocean view, so he hired local farmers to move the house in the off-season, which proved more onerous than the farmers thought. When they got both halves of the house to the right location, they couldn't

Angel of the Sea   Courtesy of Marc Steiner/Agency New Jersey

figure out how to put them back together, so they built walls on the open ends, and Weightman had two houses instead of one. You can still see where the two houses should have joined. They had been abandoned when John and Barbara Girton literally climbed through a broken window to see what was inside. Since the building reopened as the Angel of the Sea, it's been recognized as one of the top 10 bed & breakfasts in the United States. $$–$$$$.

Beach Shack (877-742-2507; beachshack.com), 205 Beach Ave., Cape May 08204. This motel used to be the Coachman, and was refurbished, refinished, and reopened in 2009 as the Beach Shack while keeping the late-'60s vibe that is considered retro cool

today. Rooms sleep four to six people. If you're bringing a larger group, consider Bungalow 2, which looks very Brady Bunch. Open early May–Columbus Day weekend. $$.

Billmae Cottage (609-898-8558; billmae.com), 1015 Washington St., Cape May 08204. Want to bring Fido along? He or she is welcome at the Billmae Cottage, and might make a few friends, too, at this "B&D"—D for "dog." The rooms are decorated in country style and include a parlor, full kitchen, and bath. Remember, this isn't a B&B, so breakfast is not part of the package, but don't miss "Yappy Hour" where B&D guests and their dogs are invited to meet and hang out on the enclosed porch with innkeepers Bob and Linda

Comfort Stations

If you need to "go" while walking around Cape May, look for a Comfort Station. That's their word for *restroom*. There's one in Washington Commons and one on Washington Square Mall.

Steenrod and their two husky/Lab mixes, Jameson and Guinness. Book this one early. Regulars make reservations many months in advance. No cats allowed. $$.

The Chalfonte Hotel (609-884-8409; chalfonte.com), 301 Howard St., Cape May 08204. In 2009 the Chalfonte finally moved into the 21st century: The owners installed central air. This hasn't altered the Victorian hotel's charm, and you can still book a room with a shared bathroom (yes, they have plenty with rooms with private baths). Make sure you stop in at the hotel's King Edward Bar. "The Eddie" is a locals' favorite. Open in-season. $$–$$$.

Hotel Alcott (800-272-3004; hotelalcott.com), 107–133 Grant St., Cape May 08204. The historic and the modern mix well at this century-plus-year-old hotel. Sure, you'll find a flat-screen TV in your room, but it's surrounded by suites recently remodeled to reflect the building's rich Victorian history. A big draw is the veranda, with its white wood railings, rocking chairs, and ocean breezes. Why Hotel Alcott? Because Louisa May Alcott, author of *Little Women*, was a frequent guest. $$$–$$$$.

The Beach Shack   Courtesy of the Beach Shack

Congress Hall

(888-944-1816; con
gresshall.com), 251
Beach Ave., Cape May
08204. There might
not be a "hotel" in the
title, but Cape May's
Congress Hall has
been serving guests in
luxury and style since
1816, with a few inter-
ruptions, including fire,
hurricanes, war, and
scores of renovations.

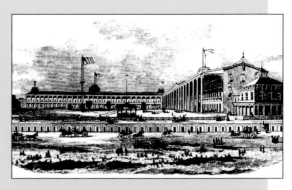

Congress Hall before the Great Fire of 1878.
Courtesy of Emil R Salvini from: *The Summer City by the Sea, An Illustrated History of Cape May, NJ* (Rutgers University Press)

As it stands today, Congress Hall is a reincarnation of its former self
with the most modern of amenities, offering visitors a first-class vacation with a laid-back, almost southern charm.

"When first built, the hotel was called the Big House by the Sea,"
says John Daily, general manager of Congress Hall. And big it was—in
1816 it had 100 rooms, which made it one of the largest hotels in the
country. Most people weren't sure how a seaside hotel would do.
Congress Hall was the first such establishment. So the townspeople
nicknamed the building "Tommy's Folly" after Thomas Hughes, who

Convention Hall beach and boardwalk circa 1930   Courtesy of Ben Miller

Bathing Beach & Boardwalk Front of Congress Hall, Cape May, N. J.

Congress Hall today   Courtesy of Congress Hall

built Congress Hall. Where does the *Congress* part come in? From 1829 to 1833 Hughes served in Congress, and his building proved to be no folly.

The original building burned down in the great fire of 1878. Within a year, Congress Hall, this time built of brick instead of wood, was back. Since then it has been the center of a bitter town feud, shut down, and reopened as the site of the first post-Prohibition cocktail bar, and part of the Cape May Bible Conference. In 1995, Curtis Bashaw and Craig Wood bought the building and brought it back to how it once looked, reopening in 2002. Many of the rooms still have vintage pieces, like claw-foot bathtubs, as well as the modern conveniences of a luxury hotel. Plus, if you're a guest, they'll bring your lunch to your beach chair. The restaurants and bars at Congress Hall bustle all season long, and the rocking chairs outside are a popular meeting spot.

Congress Hall is also home to the Sea Spa and pool, plus the Blue Pig Tavern (despite the swine-y name, it's a great place to eat) and two lounges. The Boiler Room is where its name implies—the hotel's former boiler room—and its mix of exposed walls plus stainless-steel decor and live music creates a sophisticated nightclub experience underground. You can also sip swanky cocktails in the Brown Room, which connects the lobby with the ballroom and dining rooms.

If you're a beer fan, especially microbrews, try the Blue Pig Tavern Ale. It has a light taste made for summer by New Jersey brewery Flying Fish.

I've stayed here in all seasons. Even in the dead of winter, when most of the town is buttoned up until spring, it's a charming place to be.

Inn at the Park (866-884-8406; innattheparknj.com), 1002 Washington St., Cape May 08204. The Victorian charm is not lost at this bed & breakfast, which is near the Emlen Physick estate. Enjoy a pre-dinner cocktail hour by sampling from innkeepers Jay and Mary Ann Gorrick's extensive wine collection. The rooms are cozy with just a little bit of fuss—enough to enhance the sweet romantic vibe of the inn without going overboard. When you're in the parlor, make sure to look for light coming in through the stained-glass windows. Gorgeous. $$–$$$$.

Mainstay Bed and Breakfast Inn (609-884-8690; mainstayinn .com), 635 Columbia Ave., Cape May 08204. This inn, which was designed by Philadelphia architect Stephen D. Button and built in the late 1800s, started out as a private gambling club, then became a summer residence, a guesthouse, and a bed & breakfast. A 1970s renovation brought the inn back to how it originally looked. The Mainstay also includes a cottage, which is located next door and was built by the same architect as the original portion of the Mainstay. Closed Dec.–Apr. $$$$.

Queen Victoria Bed & Breakfast (609-884-8702; queenvictoria .com), 102 Ocean St., Cape May 08204. It's not exactly one B&B at Queen Victoria—the complex is made up of four buildings. The Queen Victoria building, which has nine rooms, was built in 1881 and

Queen Victoria at Christmas   Courtesy of the Mid-Atlantic Center for the Arts & Humanities

sold in 1889 to Dr. Franklin Hughes, who leased it to the navy to use as a war camp community service building before the Hughes family returned in 1918. The House of the Royals has nine rooms and is the oldest structure on the property. It was built in 1776 by Charles Shaw, who also built the Chalfonte

Hotel and Emlen Physick Estate. The Queen's Cottage is an 1888 building and is the cottage of choice for many vacationing couples. Prince Albert Hall has six rooms and five luxury suites, all with private whirlpool tubs. The rooms, like the building, are all Victorian. $$$–$$$$.

Local Flavors

Taste of the town—local restaurants, cafés, bars, bistros, etc.

Axelsson's Blue Claw (609-884-5878; blueclawrestaurant.com), 991 Ocean Dr., Cape May 08204. This dockside restaurant comes with a five-star rating from the North American Restaurant Association. As you can imagine, the blue claw crabcakes (appetizer and entrée sizes) are a popular menu item, as are rich pasta dishes and the oyster bar. They have an impressive martini menu as well. Reservations recommended. Dinner. $$$.

Blue Pig Tavern (609-884-8422; congresshall.com), Congress Hall, 251 Beach Ave., Cape May 08204. This restaurant isn't really a tavern, and, aside from the charbroiled pork chop, doesn't have much to do with pigs. Congress Hall's in-house restaurant was named after the first tavern to come to Cape May, which was located on what is now Congress

Hall's lawn. The menu is a mix of surf-and-turf classics that lean heavily on what's in-season at the time. Eat inside or out. Breakfast, lunch, dinner. $$.

Carriage House Tearoom & Café (609-884-5111; capemay mac.org), 1048 Washington St., Cape May 08204. The Carriage House, which is part of the Emlen Physick Estate, serves classic tearoom dishes. For the complete high-tea experience, don one of the colorful and flowery hats provided by the Carriage House. BYOB. Lunch, afternoon tea in-season. Call for off-season hours. $$.

Copperfish on Broadway (609-898-0354; thecopperfishrestaurant .com), 416 S. Broadway, West Cape May 08204. It's New American cuisine at this Zagat-rated restaurant. What's New American? How about steak *frites* made with short rib, Brazilian chimichurri, and grilled asparagus? BYOB. Dinner. $$.

Dock Mike's Pancake House (609-884-2855; dockmikes.com), 1231 Rt. 109, Cape May 08204. The name here is a bit misleading. While Dock Mike's certainly dishes

The Fire

It might have happened more than 100 years ago, but people in Cape May still talk about "the fire" because it so radically changed the way the town looked.

Early on the morning of November 9, 1878, arsonists set fire to the Ocean House hotel. The fire quickly spread to Congress Hall, and then from one more wooden structure to another. Newspapers from the time say that the fire burned for better than 11 hours, and smoldered for much longer. The fire destroyed more than 35 acres of Cape May. No one was killed, and the arsonists were never caught.

The destruction of so much property called for the new building without which Cape May wouldn't have many of the Victorian bed & breakfasts that are such a draw today. If you read through the lodging section of this book, you'll see that most of the Victorian-themed buildings were constructed in the 1880s, many on the spots of the grand old (and very wooden) hotels that burned to the ground. Most residents think that a demolish-and-redevelopment craze that almost took over the town in the 1970s would have been much more devastating. I think they're right.

up pancakes in many different varieties, including sweet potato and "Mikey" Mouse, it's also a lunch spot and has more than 100 different items to try, including wraps, seafood samplers, and cheese steaks—all of which are listed on your place-mat menu. One of the few breakfast spots open year-round. No credit cards. Breakfast, lunch. $–$$.

The Ebbitt Room (609-884-5700; virginiahotel.com), Virginia Hotel, 25 Jackson St., Cape May 08204. This gourmet restaurant has received kudos from all over the country, from *The New York Times* to Zagat, which rates it as one of the best restaurants on the Jersey

The Virginia, home of the Ebbitt Room
Courtesy of the Virginia

Shore. It's *the* place to go in Cape May for a luxurious meal or special occasion. If you're not feeling up to the full luxury experience, you can sample bits of the Ebbitt Room

Porch at Gecko's

menu, like Kobe beef sliders and *pomme frites*, in the Ebbitt Room Lounge. In summer 2010 they started Farm to Table nights that allow you to experience the Ebbitt Room menu with dishes made almost entirely of local foods, for a fixed price. Reservations recommended. Dinner. $$$–$$$$.

Gecko's (609-898-7750), 31 Perry St., Cape May 08204. Make sure you sit on the deck at Gecko's. The treetop canopy makes it a shady spot just close enough to the action of Cape May to ensure inter-

esting people-watching. Chef Randy Bithell has created a southwestern menu. The Three Sister Quesadilla is a highlight, and might make you think that turning vegetarian isn't such a bad idea. BYOB. Lunch, dinner in-season. $$.

George's Place (609-884-6088), 301 Beach Ave., Cape May. George's doesn't look like much from the outside—a slip of a restaurant in the same building as a few stores. But the food is a wonder, taking traditional Greek diner fare to a more gourmet level. The

Higher Grounds Coffee Café and Natural Market

banana French toast is a specialty. No credit cards. Breakfast, lunch, dinner. $–$$.

Harpoon Henry's (609-886-5529; harpoonhenrys.net), 91 Beach Dr., North Cape May 08204. Like Teresa and Ed Henry's other Cape May restaurant, Henry's on the Beach, the view here is beautiful. Instead of beach sights, though, Harpoon Henry's overlooks Delaware Bay, which means sunset views. Build your own burger, or try a basket of something good and fried, like shrimp or chicken. They have more than 250 frozen drinks so you can sip and toast as that sun slides down. Dinner mid-Apr.–Oct. Lunch added Sat. and Sun. $$.

Henry's on the Beach (609-884-8826; henrysonthebeach.com), 702 Beach Ave., Cape May 08204. If you're worried you won't grab a beach-side seat at Henry's, don't be—the deck is huge, and is what makes Henry's a draw. The food doesn't hurt, either—the Italian bake is a perennial favorite, as is the key lime pie. If you're a late riser, Henry's has select breakfast items on the lunch menu. BYOB. Breakfast, lunch, dinner in-season. Open May–Oct. $$.

Higher Grounds Coffee Café and Natural Market (609-884-1131), 479B W. Perry St., West Cape May 08204. Get your grounds done right and organic at this West Cape May coffee shop. It's open year-round and has an outdoor garden where you can sit and chat. They're super-green too: Coffee is served in biodegradable cups, and they also dish up organic food. Open 7:30 AM–4 PM Mon.–Sat., 7–4 Sun.

Hot Dog Tommy's (609-884-8388; hotdogtommys.com), Jackson St. at Beach Ave., Cape May 08204. Sure, you could get just a hot dog here, but why not step out of norm and go for the Doc Dog, which has mustard, chili, and onions? Or the Buffalo Dog, which has Buffalo sauce, onions, and blue cheese? Or a Tornado Dog, with mashed potatoes, chili, cheese, salsa, banana peppers, and sour cream? My favorite is the Hot Dog Tommy, which includes Tabasco mayo, tomatoes, and onion. Hopefully you'll catch Tommy himself behind the counter. He's hard to miss in his hot dog hat. No seating. No credit cards. Open 9:57 AM–6:01 PM (yes, that's what Tommy asked me to write). $.

Lobster House (609-884-8296; thelobsterhouse.com), Fisherman's Wharf, Cape May Harbor, Cape May 08204. Eat right on the water—literally on the deck of a schooner—at this popular seafood spot. If you don't have the sea legs for it, don't worry. The bulk of the Lobster House's seating is indoors. Seafood is king here, both on the main restaurant menu and through the ever-popular raw bar. The specialty? Lobster, of course, which comes in the form of lobster tails or whole lobster, steamed or broiled. Don't turn aside the house bread, either. It's incredible. Expect long waits on weeknights in summer, though there is a way around the line. I visited on a Saturday night in August and arrived right at 5 PM. The restaurant had just opened, so us early birds were put into a line and seated—no wait required. An hour later, a few dozen people hung around the bar and entrance to the Lobster House for what I heard was expected to be an hour or two wait. Breakfast, lunch, dinner in-season. Call for off-season hours. $$–$$$$.

Lucky Bones Backwater Grille (609-884-BONE; luckybonesgrille .com), 1200 Rt. 109 S., Cape May 08204. This is where the locals go, which is why it's crowded even in the off-season. The menu runs

Hot Dog Tommy himself at Hot Dog Tommy's

from thick-crust brick-oven pizza to the half-pound Lucky Bones Burger. Late night features the greatest hits off the dinner menu, and the bar scene is packed. They do "Lucky to Go" curbside take-out now, too. Lunch, dinner. $$.

Mad Batter (609-884-5970; madbatter.com), Carroll Villa Hotel, 19 Jackson St., Cape May 08204. Any meal here is great, but brunch is a standout. They take American breakfast classics, like pancakes and French toast, and make them gourmet. The bar is an excellent place to stop for a drink and a meal, too. Don't skip the bloody Mary. Reservations recommended for dinner. Breakfast, lunch, dinner in-season. Weekends only Jan.–Mar. $$–$$$.

Mangia Mangia (609-884-2429; mangiamangiacapemay.com), 110 N. Broadway, West Cape May 08204. If you like pasta, and a lot of it, you'll want to make a stop at Mangia Mangia. For more than a dozen years they've been dishing up the best of the carby stuff in proportions that'll fill you for a day or more. The fried ravioli is a local favorite. BYOB. Dinner. $$.

Martini Beach (609-884-1925; martinibeachcapemay.com), 429 Beach Ave., Cape May 08204. They've got martinis and views of the beach. What more could you want? Food, of course, and Martini Beach was the first spot in Cape May to offer tapas dining. This way, you can taste the lobster mac and cheese, sesame tuna, and calamari

Exit Zero

Make sure to pick up a copy of *Exit Zero* while you're in town. It's a free, weekly black-and-white newspaper started by Jack Wright, a former New York City magazine editor who came to Cape May to write a book about Congress Hall and never left. He's created a publishing company that not only includes *Exit Zero* (which is an excellent mix of journalism and events coverage), but also a store and a book publishing company. If you have a copy of *Cool Cape May* in your hotel or bed & breakfast room, that's an *Exit Zero* production, too.

in one meal. You can't beat the view—Martini Beach is upstairs, so you can overlook the beach while you nosh or sip. Reservations recommended. Dinner, late night in-season. Call for off-season hours. $$.

McGlade's on the Pier (609-884-2614), 722 Beach Ave., Cape May 08204. If you're an omelet fan, you must stop here. McGlade's has more than 20 kinds on the menu, and was named omelet queen by *The New York Times*. If you're feeling adventurous, try the Mickey omelet, which has lump crab, sprouts, and avocado. If eggs aren't your thing, McGlade's has other menu options, like crabcakes and filet. Open Mother's Day–Columbus Day. $.

Peter Shields Inn & Restaurant (800-355-6565; peter shieldsinn.com), 1301 Beach Dr., Cape May 08204. The views are almost as good as the food at this ocean-sized restaurant. The menu is New American cuisine with items like smoked duck duet, seafood tapas, and rocket salad (a mix of baby arugula, toasted hazelnuts, sweet-and-sour beets, feta, and tomatoes) plus seaside classics like lobster crabcake and bouillabaisse. No children or infants. My father had his wedding here in 2008. It's a fine, romantic spot. BYOB. Dinner. Open Sat.–Sun. only in winter. Dinner. $$$.

Pilot House (609-884-3449; pilothousecapemay.com), 142 Decatur St., Cape May 08204. The Pilot House is that hole-in-the-wall with good food, a worn bar, and the same cluster of guys at their designated bar stools, except the Pilot House isn't a hole-in-the-wall but smack in the middle of Cape May. That doesn't take away from its

Cape May beach   Courtesy of Marc Steiner/Agency New Jersey

Cape May Saved

The fire of 1878 almost did in Cape May. It destroyed about 30 blocks of the town. Cape May almost faced the same fate in the 1970s, but from a different source: progress.

Cape May wasn't always known a haven of Victorian architecture. Just 30 years ago, the buildings were seen as old and worn down, roadblocks to the forward progress of the city. Developers wanted to knock them down and put up what you'll see through most other shore towns: bland, characterless condos and duplexes meant to draw vacationers for a week or two. But local citizens bent on saving these gorgeous buildings started to fight back.

Convention Hall circa 1930   Courtesy of Ben Miller

The idea of saving the history of the town started in 1959 when Cape May celebrated its 350th anniversary. The same year, the National Trust for Historic Preservation had their annual meeting in Cape May, giving an extra push to people who wanted Cape May to keep the buildings. It was a battle that stretched through the 1960s.

In 1962 a nor'easter destroyed the boardwalk, Convention Hall, and a lot of properties in Cape May. In

Convention Hall circa 1970   Courtesy of Ben Miller

1965 the town was awarded an Urban Renewal Grant to replace the boardwalk with a seawall and promenade, protecting many of the remaining Victorian buildings from the threat of flood or storm damage. The grant required that Cape May catalog their historic buildings. Carolyn Pitts headed the Historic American Buildings Survey Team, and in 1970 Pitts, along with Edwin C. Bramble of the Cape May Cottagers Association, filed for all of Cape May to be made a National

Historic Landmark, therefore saving the buildings left. They did so without the approval of Cape May's mayor, congressman, or the governor of New Jersey.

The decision couldn't be reversed, and many of the buildings that you see in Cape May were saved by the ruling. Also in 1970s, a group of volunteers saved the Emlen Physick Estate and formed the Mid-Atlantic Center for the Arts & Humanities (MAC). The tide had clearly turned against developers—Bruce Minnix, leader of MAC, was elected the next mayor. MAC now runs most of Cape May's Victorian and cultural events and has offices inside the Emlen Physick Estate.

After being saved, many buildings were converted into B&Bs. They were more economically feasible operations than summer homes. While the Victorian homes are gorgeous, they are difficult to maintain, especially if you're only using them for three months a year, if that. The town soon started offering walking tours, then horse and carriage rides. Now you can't turn around without seeing or hearing about some kind of Victorian-themed event.

locals-only feel, especially in the off-season. The food is classic, simple, and good, with selections like seafood pasta, Cape May crabcake, and London broil. They have a kids' menu, too, if you're bringing the tykes. Lunch, dinner. $$.

The Rusty Nail (609-884-0017; beachshack.com/rusty-nail.php), 205 Beach Ave., Cape May 08204. "The Nail" has long been a lifeguard hangout on the site of the Coachman Inn. When the Coachman became the Beach Shack in 2009, the Rusty Nail was renovated into *the* summer hangout in Cape May—and it still has the longest bar in town. Drink beer out of cold frosted mugs, order clams by the dozen to eat on a picnic table, or try their burger sliders in the

indoor restaurant. Live music in-season. Breakfast, lunch, dinner. Open early May–Columbus Day weekend. $$.

Ugly Mug (609-884-3459; uglymugenterprises.com), 426 Washington St., Cape May 08204. The food is good and hearty at this longtime Cape May staple. No need to dress up—just come as you are, and enjoy. It's mostly American bar food, though the restaurant is family-friendly before 9 PM, so don't worry if you're bringing the kids. Every August, Ugly Mug hosts a froth blowing contest, which is exactly what it sounds like: a contest to determine who can blow the most froth out of their ugly mug of beer. Silly hats are optional and encouraged. A great

Ceiling mugs at the Ugly Mug. Mugs pointed to sea belonged to people who have passed away.

place to watch whatever Philadelphia or New York sporting event is important to you. Lunch, dinner, late night. $.

Washington Inn (609-884-5697; washingtoninn.com), 801 Washington St., Cape May 08204. Washington Inn started as a plantation home in 1840. Today it's one of the most elegant dining experiences in Cape May. While the main menu

Promenade circa 1970 *Courtesy of Ben Miller*

might tempt you to fill your stomach with the likes of herb-crusted New Zealand rack of lamb and five-spice grilled Long Island duck breast, leave room for dessert. It's a luxurious experience. In spring and fall the inn also offers wine cellar dinners. What better place to hold them than at Washington Inn, which has more than 10,000 bottles? Proper dress required. Dinner. Call for off-season hours. $$$.

Zoe's Beachfront Eatery (609-884-1233; zoescapemay.com), Beach & Stockton Pl., Cape May 08204. This super-casual restaurant across the street from the promenade is the perfect spot for a quick summer breakfast or lunch. Not only do they have kid-friendly options and portions, but their patio is dog-friendly, too. Open breakfast and lunch Apr.–Oct. Cash only. $.

Don't Miss This

Check out these great
attractions and activities . . .

A Place on Earth (866-400-SOAP; aplaceonearth.com), 526 Washington Street Mall, Cape May 08204. All the soaps sold in this basement shop are organic, and they're hand-cut and -packaged in Cape May, so you know nothing funny's mixed in. With more than 40 flavors, A Place on Earth is sure to have something that pleases your nose. Check out the Sugar Scrub bar—a perfect way to exfoliate and revive your skin. Open 10 AM–10 PM in-season. Call for off-season hours.

Bay Springs Farm (609-884-0563; bayspringsalpacas.com), 542 New England Rd., Cape May 08204. Barbara Nuessle liked to knit, especially with yarn made from the fleece of alpacas. When she and husband Warren retired, they opted for Cape May and a brood of their own alpacas. Now the couple raises and breeds these animals, which look like small llamas, on this 10-acre farm. It's open to the public on weekends. Check out the animals, and how Barbara spins their fleece into yarn, which she uses for sweaters, scarves, blankets, and a host of other alpaca gear all sold in the farm store. Open 10 AM–4 PM Sat.–Sun. and by appointment. $.

The Bird House of Cape May (609-898-8871; birdhouseofcapemay .com), 109 Sunset Blvd., West Cape May 08204. Cape May is a bird-

Birding

Cape May is known as a romantic place, but it's also one of the most popular spots in the world for birders.

Cape May is a common stopping area from birds migrating to and from the Caribbean and South America. In fall and spring, birds rest here, and birders come to watch them. It's such a popular spot that the World Series of Birding ends here. Competitors hoping to spot the most types of birds start in northern New Jersey and end in Cape May, 24 hours later.

Birding in Cape May
Courtesy of Marc Steiner/Agency New Jersey

Where to go? Cape May State Point Park is one place—it's the southernmost tip of the state. The Cape May Bird Observatory: The Northwood Center, is another. If you're looking for more guidance with your viewing, head up to the Wetlands Institute in Stone Harbor. There you can watch from the inside in bad weather, and they have exhibits for kids.

Alpacas

At first, I didn't believe what she said.

"You're going to see the alpaca farm, right?" asked Mary Ann Gorrick over breakfast. I was staying at the Inn at the Park, which she runs with her husband, Jay.

"Excuse me?" I asked, almost choking on my pancake.

"Oh, yes, the alpacas. We'll call them and say you're coming over," she said.

Yes, there is an alpaca farm located in Cape May, which is better known for its Victorian buildings than for its livestock populations. But as I pulled up to Bay Springs Farm, there they were, these mini llamas, curious about the newcomer.

Fernando, a young, black alpaca, bounded right up to the gate to meet me. Warren Nuessle waved me over and said it was okay to pet Fernando, but only on his back.

Barbara Nuessle had always been a knitter, and she loved working with the yarn that was spun from alpaca fleece. So when she and Warren were looking what to do when they retired, alpacas came to the top of the list.

They moved from Bryn Mawr, Pennsylvania, to Cape May. Nuessle still makes things from the alpaca fleece, and she spins the yarn herself. The goods are sold in the farmhouse store. They also breed and sell alpacas, and tried to convince me that they make good pets. It's not that I don't believe them, but I barely have enough space for a 12-pound dog. Still, I wouldn't mind having my dog go to the bathroom in the same spot all the time, which is what alpacas do.

Bay Springs Farm

Cape May Lighthouse circa 1950   Courtesy of Ben Miller

watching hot spot, and this shop caters to those who come to town to see what's flying through. Most of the stock is items designed to draw the little birdies to your backyard. Open 10 AM–5 PM.

Cape May Bird Observatory: The North-wood Center (609-884-2736; njaudubon.org), 701 E. Lake Dr., Cape May Point 08204. Cape May's location at the tip of the state along the Atlantic Flyway makes it a resting spot for birds, and the folks at Northwood Center will help you find them. You can join in on a daily walk or hire a guide for a private tour. Don't worry if you forgot your binoculars—you can rent them here as well. If the hours seem wonky to you, remember that peak time for birding is in spring and fall. Open 9:30 AM–4:30 PM Apr.–May and Sept.–Nov. Call for off-season hours.

Cape May Fire Department Museum (609-884-9512; capemayfd.com/museum.htm), 643 Washington St., Cape May 08204. Indulge your child-hood fantasy about growing up to be a firefighter at this museum. Like most things in Cape May, it's from the Victorian era, and the fire engine inside is a 1928 American Lafrance. Open 8 AM–9 PM. Free.

Cape May Lighthouse (800-275-4278; capemaymac.org), 104 Lincoln Ave., Cape May Point 08212. This still-active lighthouse is the third to light the tip of Cape May (two others were lost to erosion). It was built in 1859 at just over 156 feet tall, with 218 steps. You can walk up them all by yourself for unparalleled views from the southern tip of New Jersey, but be warned—it's a hike up to the top and back down, so if you're not looking to sweat on your trip, then enjoy the gift shop at the base, or visit when the keeper gives a half-hour talk about the lighthouse and what his job is like. Open daily Apr.–Nov. Call for off-season hours. $.

Cape May Linen Outlet (866-884-3630; capemaylinen.com), 110 Park Blvd., West Cape May 08204. Dress your house for less at this outlet shop. They stock goods for your bed, bath, and kitchen at knockout prices. Open 10 AM–6 PM.

Cape May Stage (609-884-1341; capemaystage.com), 31 Perry St., Cape May 08204. Classic, traditional, contemporary and new theater

The Light of Asia

Lucy wasn't always the only wooden elephant to grace the sands of the Jersey Shore. The Light of Asia was her cousin (and last elephant of a trio—the other was in Coney Island), and, once completed in 1884, stood watch in Cape May. The locals, though, called her Jumbo.

Her tenure hasn't been as successful as that of Lucy, who still stands in Margate. The Light of Asia was dismantled in 1900.

LIGHT OF ASIA.

productions all find a home at this professional Equity theater. The Robert Shackleton Playhouse is small and cozy, so you'll feel almost part of the play. The annual holiday shows are some of the most popular. Many of Cape May's restaurants participate in "Dinner and a Show," where you'll enjoy specials on ticket prices or food. $$.

Cape May Miniature Golf Club & Cocomoe's (609-884-2222), 315 Jackson St., Cape May 08204. This course has 18 holes, water hazards, and real—yes, real—sand traps to make for a tricky shore mini golf tradition. After your round, stop in at Cocomoe's, the attached ice cream parlor that offers 24 flavors of ice cream plus Italian ice, smoothies, yogurt, shakes, and, if you're really hungry, banana splits. In-season the golf club is open 10 AM–10:30 PM; Cocomoe's, 11–11.

Cape May Point State Park (609-884-2159; state.nj.us/dep/parksand forests/parks/capemay.html), 299 Light House Ave., Cape May Point 08204. The Cape May Lighthouse isn't the only thing at Cape May's point. It's also home to nature trails, bird-watching areas, and this museum, which showcases New Jersey wildlife and the history of Cape May, including a map that shows what areas have been lost to beach erosion. Some of the birding trails are wheelchair accessible, too. If you'd like a guide to show you what's what, just ask—the tours are free, but you must schedule them in advance. Open dawn–dusk. Free.

Cape May Whale Watcher (800-786-5445; capemaywhalewatcher .com), 2nd Ave. and Wilson Dr., Cape May 08204. More than 500 dolphins live in Cape May's waters from spring through fall, and a great way to see them while being taught about Cape May's nautical past is by taking a ride with the Cape May Whale Watcher. Best time to see whales is in fall. A sighting of whales or dolphins is guaranteed, or you'll get a coupon for a free ride. Cape May Whale Watcher runs dinner cruises, too. Cruises at 10 AM, 1 PM, and 6:30 PM. Open Mar.–Dec. $$–$$$.

Cape May Winery & Vineyard (609-884-1169; capemaywinery.com), 711 Townbank Rd., Cape May 08204. An ideal setting to sip local wines: Sit on the deck of the Cape May Vineyard headquarters, or take your picnic out on the lawn. This vineyard is the southernmost in New Jersey, and its temperatures are moderated by the ocean, which helps them produce a lot of top-quality wines, including Chardonnay, Riesling, Merlot, Cabernet Franc, and Cabernet Sauvignon. Winemaking tours are also available. Tasting room open noon–6 PM June–Sept., noon–5 off-season. $.

Celebrate Cape May (609-884-9032), 315 Ocean St., Cape May NJ. If you need something with CAPE MAY written on it, stop here. From shirts to hats to bumper stickers to postcards to lighthouses, this store in the Washington Commons shops will have it for you. Open 9:30 AM–11 PM in-season. Call for off-season hours.

Cheeks (866-5-CHEEKS; cheekscapemay.com), 101 Ocean St., Cape May 08204. This 20-plus-year-old story specializes in cool, comfy, breezy flax linen clothing, though they also offer shoes, gifts, soaps, and cards in the attached gift store. If you're looking for a steal, check out their warehouse store at 600 Park Blvd. in West Cape May: Prices are knocked down 20 to 40 percent. Open 10 AM–6 PM.

Higbee Beach

If you're a birder, you know Higbee Beach. Located on the western side of Cape May—on Delaware Bay—it's one of the most popular spots to sight birds in the state.

Until 1999 it was also famous for another type of sighting: Higbee was a nude beach. For decades people came to sunbathe here au naturel. But complaints of so-called lewd behavior led to the state banning the practice. After a lot of protests and questions as to whether Upper Townships could enforce a ban (Higbee is on state property), the ruling stands today, and you must wear your bathing suit at Higbee.

It's also dog-friendly. I take my Jack Russell terrier, Emily, to Higbee whenever I can. The waves aren't big, which is just her speed. It's hard to pull her away once she gets in the water. Make sure you bring plenty of bags with you if you bring your dog, and always keep him or her on a leash.

Emlen Physick Estate   Courtesy of the Mid-Atlantic Center for the Arts & Humanities

Dellas 5 & 10 (609-884-4568), 503 Washington St., Cape May 08204. Dellas is the place to stop for all those little things you forgot to bring (my best buy was a $5 bikini), or souvenirs to take home as a reminder of your Jersey Shore trip. Browsing is fun, too, since Dellas has a retro '40s and '50s feel. They also have a diner counter in the back. Open 8 AM–10 PM in-season. Call for off-season hours.

East Lynne Theater Company (609-884-5898; eastlynnetheater.org), First Presbyterian Church, 500 Hughes St., Cape May 08204. You'll see American classics and world premieres through this theater company, which performs at the First Presbyterian Church of Cape May. They also take their talents into the town by performing short stories on the porches and verandas of Cape May's inns and B&Bs. $$.

Emlen Physick Estate (800-275-4278; capemaymac.org), 1048 Washington St., Cape May 08204. In 1879, Emlen Physick built an 18-room mansion in Cape May, which was just starting to become a seaside resort. He liked it so much that Physick moved to Cape May from Philadelphia, bringing his mother and aunt with him. The estate had fallen into disrepair by 1970, when it was saved by what's now called the Mid-Atlantic Center for the Arts & Humanities. They've restored the building, designed by famed Philadelphia architect Frank Furness, to just about how it looked with the Physicks lived there. Ask to see the corner left untouched in the formal parlor—you can see what terrible shape the building had been in. Guided tours are available year-round. Tour times vary throughout the year; children's tours are also available. Tours daily Apr.–Dec. and weekends Jan.–Mar. Call for tour times. $.

Flying Fish Studio (800-639-2085; theflyingfishstudio.com), 130 Park Blvd., West Cape May 08204. Who needs another boring HERE'S WHERE I WENT ON VACATION T-shirt? You won't find that at Flying Fish—they make catchy beach-themed gear, like sweatshirts with a big lobster on the front, or retro-designed shirts dedicated to Cape May's smaller beaches, like Poverty Beach. I'm partial to the octopus prints. They also provide gear for the annual Lima Bean Festival, plus all those fashion extras you might have forgotten, including flip-flops, wedges, hats, and organic cotton tees, all at affordable prices. Open 10 AM–5 PM.

Historic Cold Spring Village (609-898-2300; hcsv.org), 720 Rt. 9 S., Cape May 08204. Don't roll your eyes. Historic Cold Spring Village is *not* a boring history lesson. It can be a relaxing outdoor stroll (they have 22 acres of land), an arts-and-crafts shopping spree (artists work in the village through the country store), or a cooking trip (you can take in a 19th-century cooking demonstration). Of course, you can make your visit a history lesson about life in the 19th century, but whether it's boring depends on you. Open 10 AM–4:30 PM Sat.–Sun., late May–late June; 10–4:30 Tue.–Sun. late June–early Sept.; 10–4:30 on weekends until mid-Sept. $.

Love the Cook (609-884-9292; lovethecook.com), 404 Washington Street Mall, Cape May 08204. Do you need a Buddha bowl? What about a gurgling fish jug? You'll find what you never knew you were looking for at this kitchen specialty shop, along with spices, rubs, and gourmet coffees and teas. Open 10 AM–10:30 PM in-season. Call for off-season hours.

Cape May Diamonds

A Cape May diamond isn't really a diamond. It's a pure quartz crystal from the Delaware River that has been rounded and smoothed by its 200-mile journey, which ends at Sunset Beach.

You can find them on your own while waiting for sunset, or buy one that's been tumbled clear and set into jewelry at the Sunset Beach Gift Shop.

Mary Ann's Jewelry (609-898-8786), 511 Washington Street Mall, Cape May 08204. Don't overlook this galley-sized store. It stocks both estate and new jewelry, including engagement and wedding bands. They buy jewelry, too, and sell antiques. On one trip to Mary Ann's, I found a stunning red glass antique mirror. Perfect for trying on jewelry—better in your home. Open 10 AM–10 PM in-season. Call for off-season hours.

Nature Center of Cape May (609-898-8848; njaudubon.org/centers/nccm), 1600 Delaware Ave., Cape May 08204. The Nature Center of Cape May is the place to go to learn about the habitat surrounding your vacation

Horseshoe Crab

No horseshoe crab ever won a beauty contest. Every time I see one or its shell, my reaction is to walk away with an "Eww."

Horseshoe crabs are an ancient species, older than dinosaurs, and Delaware Bay is the world's largest spawning grounds for them. The Delaware Estuary is also the largest staging area of shorebirds that travel the Atlantic Flyway, largely due to horseshoe crabs—birds eat their eggs. Horseshoe crabs can also save your life, indirectly. According to the Ecological Research and Development Group, extract of blood from horseshoe crabs is used to make sure that items like intravenous drugs, vaccines, and medical devices are bacteria-free.

You can get up close and personal with horseshoe crabs at the **Nature Center of Cape May** (609-898-8848, njaudubon.org/centers/nccm; 1600 Delaware Ave., Cape May). You can run your finger along its body, claws and all. It's was the easiest way to see that horseshoe crabs aren't dangerous at all. A pinch is more like a love tap—that's how weak their claws are.

If you see one on the beach, it's usually just a shell. But if there happens to be one alive inside, leave the old guy or gal alone, or flip it over so that it can go back into the water. They couldn't harm a fly, but they help a lot of people and critters, so you're doing yourself a favor by letting it live on.

spot. Kids will enjoy the hands-on activities, like a touch tank, or daylong camp projects, and everyone in your group can enjoy family programs such as bike tours and harbor safaris. Open 10 AM–1 PM Tue.–Sat., Jan.–Feb.; 10–3 Tue.–Sat., Mar.–May; 9–4 daily, June–Aug.; 10–3 Tue.–Sat., Sept.–Dec. Events $–$$.

Naval Air Station Wildwood Aviation Museum (609-886-8787; usnasw .org), 500 Forrestal Rd., Rio Grande 08204. Check out World War II aircraft at this museum, which is located inside the Cape May County Airport. The airport itself used to be a naval air base during World War II, and it's where pilots learned to fly the SB2C Helldiver. You can check out the Helldiver, F14 Tomcat, UH-1 Huey, and T-33 Thunderbird, among others. Open 9 AM–5 PM in-season; call for off-season hours. $.

Stitch by Stitch (866-563-5399; stitchbystitchnj.com), 315 Ocean St., Unit 9, Cape May 08204. Needleworkers, delight! You can find just about any pattern you would ever want to cross-stitch in this charming shop. They sell kits, patterns, and yarn for cross-stitching, and also kits to make beaded jewelry. If they don't have what you're looking for, ask. They'll know where to get it. Open 10 AM–10 PM in-season, 10–5 off-season.

Sunset Beach Flag Ceremony (sunsetbeachnj.com), Sunset Beach, Cape May Point. Take in the sunset at this beach, which is the southernmost part of New Jersey, and one of the few places on the East Coast where you can see the sun set over the ocean (as opposed to rise). Flags flown here are those from the graves of American veterans, and "God Bless America" is played every night as the sun sets. It's not a solemn ceremony, though. It's more like a party to celebrate a great beach day. Memorial Day–Labor Day. Free.

Swede Things in America (609-884-5811; swedethings.com), 307 Washington Street Mall, Cape May 08204. You'll find the best of Sweden in this quaint shop, including china, crystal, and lamps. The lace goods are a big draw, and they last—all the pretty lace runners and curtains in my mother's house are from Swede Things, and holding strong after 25 years. Open 10 AM–10 PM in-season. Call for off-season hours.

Turdo Vineyards & Winery (609-884-5591; turdovineyards.com), 3911 Bayshore Rd., North Cape May 08204. Turdo Vineyards makes 12 different kinds of wine, many of which have won state awards, and they invite you inside to take a look at how it's done. Open noon–5 PM Memorial Day–Labor Day; noon–5 Thu.–Sat. off-season. $.

Victorious (609-898-1777; victorious antiques.com), Congress Hall, 251 Beach Ave., Cape May 08204. Browse through new and estate jewelry and decor, which are nestled among Victoriana. The Congress Hall location has more estate jewelry than the Stone Harbor outpost, which is mostly re-creations. Victorious also has a location at 315 Ocean St. in Cape May. Open 10 AM–10 PM.

Wave One Sports (609-884-6674; waveonesports.com), 324 Washington Street Mall, Cape May 08204. They don't sell just any old Cape May gear at Wave One. Their items, which range from embroidered sweatshirts to hats to T-shirts to sweatpants, are high quality and last for years (I have three of their sweatshirts older than my college degree, if that says anything). Open 9 AM–11 PM in-season. Call for off-season hours.

Swede Things

Whale's Tale (609-884-4808; whalestalecapemay.com), 312 Washington Street Mall, Cape May 08204. Whale's Tale is the kind of place that has something for everyone, but not in that cheap dollar-store way. It's full of possibilities, from the jewelry counter that sits in the middle of the front room to the puppet tower in the kids' section to the cards and Christmas ornaments. They stock a heavy supply of locally themed books, too. Open 10 AM–11 PM in-season. Call for off-season hours.

Winterwood Gift and Christmas Gallery (609-884-8949; winterwood gift.com), 526 Washington Street Mall, Cape May 08204. It's all Christmas all the time in this two-story shop dedicated to the holiday season. You'll find any kind of ornament you ever dreamed of for your tree, plus beach-themed decor, jewelry, and even Halloween decorations. Winterwood also has locations in Rio Grande and Wildwood. Open 9:30 AM–10 PM in-season. Call for off-season hours.

The Zoo Company (609-884-8181), 421 Washington Street Mall, Cape May 08204. These are the real deal. The Zoo Company sells plushes and puppets of licensed characters, meaning that the Elmo or Dora or Cookie Monster you get is the authentic thing, not a knockoff. Zoo Company also stocks marionettes, people puppets, and Hello Kitty items. Open 10 AM–11 PM in-season. Call for off-season hours.

48 Hours

DAY 1 Start your morning with breakfast at George's. It's a small Greek restaurant tucked into in a strip of stores, but with knockout food. Then head to the Cape May Whale Watcher for a trip that will bring you to whales or dolphins—or else you get a coupon for a free trip. Then for lunch, I implore you to stand in line for a hot dog at Hot Dog Tommy's. It's worth the wait. My choice is the Hot Dog Tommy, which has Tabasco mayo, tomatoes, and onions. Tommy most likely will be behind the counter. He's chatty, funny, wearing a ridiculous hot dog hat, and will brighten your day.

Since there's no seating at Hot Dog Tommy's, take your hot dog to a bench on the promenade to watch the people and ocean go by. Then take a stroll down the Washington Street Mall, which has stores that sell almost whatever you're looking for, from antiques (Mary Ann's Jewelry) to toys (The Zoo Company) to Swedish imports (Swede Things).

Now take a drive out to West Cape May to visit the Bay Springs Farm—a working alpaca farm. You can visit with the flock, or shop in the farm store where owner Barbara Nuessle sells items she makes from alpaca fleece.

Washington Street Mall Courtesy of Marc Steiner/Agency New Jersey

Ready for dinner? Stop in at the Brown Room at Congress Hall first for a cocktail—take your drink to one of the outdoor rocking chairs if it's nice outside. Then head to dinner. Going fancy? Then try The Ebbitt Room. A little more casual? Then Martini Beach is for you. Or if you just want great bar food with whatever sport you follow on TV, it's to the Ugly Mug.

Get in that dinner early if you want to catch a show at Cape May Stage. And trust me—you do.

The Brown Room at Congress Hall
Courtesy of Congress Hall

DAY 2

Start day 2 with a trip to the top of the Cape May Lighthouse or, if heights aren't your thing, one of the nature trails nearby. Some are boardwalked if you're looking for a wheelchair-accessible trail. Once you've worked up an appetite, head to Dock Mike's for breakfast—a great choice year-round and one of the few breakfast spots open in winter. Then head to the Nature Center of Cape May to learn about what makes this town at the tip of the state so ecologically unique.

For lunch, stop in at Zoe's Beachfront Eatery, which is casual and good—and dog-friendly, too! If you're traveling with your pet, you'll want to

Sinks Like a Concrete Ship

It might not be the lost city, but there is an *Atlantus* by the shores of Cape May. She's a concrete ship off Sunset Beach in Cape May.

Yes, you read that right: a concrete ship. Steel shortages during World War I led the US government to experiment with different ship-building materials, and while concrete might not seem like a viable option, whoever floated the idea was on to something. The government built 38 concrete ships, 12 of which were put into service.

At the time of her construction, *Atlantus* weighed 3,000 tons and was 250 feet long. She served as a coal steamer for a year, and was decommissioned at the end of World War I.

In 1926, *Atlantus* was towed to Cape May. She'd already been stripped and bought by a salvage company, so there wasn't much of her left. She was going to be put into service as the base for a bridge, but while she awaited her fate, a storm knocked her out of her moorings, and she found her way onto the beach. She was so heavy that no one could move her, so there she stayed. You can still see her today, but she's not exactly on shore anymore. Erosion has shorted the coastline, so she's out in the water, close enough to be viewed from the shore.

Atlantus at Sunset Beach

head out to Higbee Beach, which allows dogs. Just make sure Rover is on a leash, and that you have plenty of baggies.

Stop at the Flying Fish Studio on your way back from Higbee. They don't sell just any Cape May T-shirts and sweatshirts. These are creative and fun.

If you're not interested in dog beaches (or even if you are), you must stop at the Emlen Physick Estate for a tour. It's the best way to see Cape

Cape May Lighthouse

May's history, and learn how close all those Victorian buildings came to being torn down.

Before dinner tonight, grab a beer in a frosted mug at the Rusty Nail, which has the longest bar in Cape May and has forever been a lifeguard hangout. And it's not a trip to Cape May without a trip to the Lobster House. Be prepared to wait if you don't arrive right when they open for dinner. Too crowded there? Try Lucky Bones across the street.

But make sure you eat in time, or wait to eat, so that you can catch sunset at Sunset Beach. If you're stopping there between Memorial and Labor Day, you'll see the Flag Lowering Ceremony, which honors veterans and specifically one vet whose casket flag has flown all day. While you're waiting for the sun to drop, hunt around in the sand for a Cape May Diamond—actually quartz that has been smoothed by travel and time. You can also buy one polished and set into jewelry at the Sunset Beach Gift Shop nearby.

Extend Your Stay

If you have more time, try these great places to see and things to do . . .

The Cape May Whale Watcher runs special, all-day lighthouse tours that bring you to all nine water-access-only Delaware Bay lighthouses. These cannot be seen from shore, so this is the only way you'll get a look. They mean it when they say all day—six to seven hours—so plan accordingly.

To sit and relax with a cup of organic coffee, check out Higher Grounds Coffee Café and Natural Market. They have an outdoor seating area for nicer days. If you see yarn knitted around part of the fence that marks that area, you've encountered the work of the Salty Knits, an anonymous band of knitters who, under the cover of night, knit their way around fences, trees, and signposts. It's a fun movement that splashed color around West Cape May after a grueling 2010 storm season and inspired copycats around the country.

Special Events

Festivals, parties, and happenings down the shore

January

Burns Supper (609-770-8479; exit zero.us). This annual fund-raiser for Cape May Stage is run by Jack Wright, Scotsman and publisher of *Exit Zero*. It's an homage to the national poet of Scotland, and full of whiskey, bagpipes, kilts, and haggis.

March

Sherlock Holmes Weekend (800-275-4278; capemaymac.org). Each Sherlock Holmes Weekend starts with a mystery. Then, if you're playing along, you spend the weekend trying to solve said mystery. Costumes are encouraged, and there's a $250 grand prize plus a slew of other gifts for winners. This weekend is held in both March and November.

Cape May Singer Songwriter Weekend (sscapemay.com). This weekend event brings singer-songwriters from around the country to Cape May for one of the biggest off-season events of the year.

Cape May Area Trolley Tours

No need to hurt your feet while exploring all Cape May has to offer. Take one of the town's many trolley tours, all operated by the Mid-Atlantic Center for the Arts & Humanities. There's the classic Historic District Trolley, the Welcome to Cape May Trolley Tour, and the ever-romantic Evening Trolley Tour. But you can get much more specific with the following tour types:

- Children's Trolley Tour
- Ghosts of Cape May Trolley Tour
- Holiday Season Evening Trolley Tour
- Natural Habitats Trolley Tour
- Spirit of the Light Trolley Tours
- US Coast Guard Base Trolley Tour
- World War II Trolley Tour

Check in with the Mid-Atlantic Center for the Arts & Humanities about tours, times, and spots to board—and keep in mind that some

Trolley tour
Courtesy of the Mid-Atlantic Center for the Arts & Humanities

of these tours are seasonal. They can be reached at 609-884-5404 or at capemaymac.org.

Ocean Drive Marathon (609-523-0880; odmarathon.com). Take in the shore sites through this spring marathon, which starts in Cape May and ends in Sea Isle City. The course is all on paved roads or boardwalk. If you're not quite up to 26.2 miles, you can also try a 10-miler, a 5k (3.1 miles), or a 1.5-mile fun run and walk.

April

Cape May's Spring Festival (800-275-4278; capemaymac.org). This town-wide event welcomes warmer temperatures and celebrates Cape May's Victorian heritage in a 10-day combination outdoor and historical festival. Free.

May

Cape May Music Festival (800-275-4278; capemaymac.org). For four weeks every spring, Cape May plays host to music performance from orchestras, jazz players, and brass bands. Concerts are held at the Cape May Convention Hall, Beach Drive at Stockton Place, or the Episcopal Church of the Advent. $.

World Series of Birding (609-884-2736; worldseriesofbirding.org). This 24-hour bird-watching competition (how many can you identify in one day?) starts in North Jersey and ends up in Cape May. Yes, you can participate, even if you didn't know that *seagull* isn't an appropriate term to describe any bird.

June

NJ State Film Festival (609-884-6700; njstatefilmfestival.com). Take in short films, documentaries, and independent flicks from all over the New Jersey at this state festival. Film students can sign up for workshops, classes, or a five-day summer institute that runs parallel to the film festival. Tickets can be purchased per film or in packages. $$–$$$$.

West Cape May Strawberry Festival (609-884-8382; westcapemay today.com). They don't call it the Garden State for nothing. Eat strawberries straight up, built into strawberry shortcake, or any of the other dozens of ways local farmers and chefs have figured out how to use this berry for your benefit.

August

Baby Parade, Beach Avenue, Cape May. Think your kid's the cutest? Then enter him or her into this long-running baby parade. Or just watch the cute kids go by. Free.

Railroad Days (609-898-2300; hcsv.org), Historic Cold Spring Village. If the choo-choos get you going, then check out this two-day event that includes demonstrations by garden railroad groups, working scale-model railroads, and displays of train memorabilia. $.

September

Revolutionary War Encampment (609-898-2300; hcsv.org), Historic Cold Spring Village. Take a peek at Revolutionary War life at this reenactment, where you can see how soldiers in 1775 lived, slept, ate, and trained. $.

Cape May Food and Wine Festival (800-275-4278; capemaymac.org). If you love to cook, or just eat, come to town in September for his event. You can take classes and seminars, tour the kitchens of Cape May restaurants, and vote for your favorite clam chowder. Or just eat. And eat. And eat.

October

West Cape May Lima Bean Festival (609-884-8382; westcapemaytoday .com). Don't grimace. They really don't taste bad, so give the mighty lima bean another chance (or taste again) at this annual festival. Don't forget to stick around for the crowning of the Bean Queen and King. Free.

Halloween in Cape May (800-275-4278; capemaymac.org). From mid-October through to the big day, Cape May embraces its haunted past. You'll find ghost tours, psychic teas, and, new in 2010, a murder mystery performance at the Emlen Physick Estate.

Victorian Week (800-275-4278; capemaymac.org). This week is actually 10 days long and features tours and events including Victorian feasts, murder mystery dinners, Victorian fashion shows, and glassblowing demonstrations.

November

Cape May Jazz Festival (609-884-7277; capemayjazz.org). Jazz takes over the town for a weekend in November with shows all over Cape May. If you want to do more than just listen, sign up for one of the workshops that set up during the week—or if you've got at least one year of playing time under your belt, the jazz improv session.

Sherlock Holmes Weekend (800-275-4278; capemaymac.org). Each Sherlock Holmes Weekend starts with a mystery. Then, if you're playing along, you spend the weekend trying to solve said mystery. Costumes are encouraged, and there's a $250 grand prize plus a slew of other gifts for winners. This weekend is held in both March and November.

December

Annual Holiday Show (609-884-1341; capemaystage.com), Cape May Stage. Every holiday season, the Cape May Stage puts on a Christmas-

Cape May–Lewes Ferry

1-800-643-3779
www.capemaylewesferry.com

Just because New Jersey ends in Cape May doesn't mean the country does, and an easy way to keep moving south is via the Cape May–Lewes Ferry. It's a cheap boating thrill to ride across the bay from the tip of our state to the edge of the smallest guy in the union. A trip takes about 80 minutes. A shuttle bus is available on the Delaware side that includes stops at the Rehoboth Beach Outlet Centers, should you want to enjoy Delaware's tax-free shopping. You can also bring your car on board, though it'll cost you. Make reservations beforehand—the ferry's car spots fill up quickly.

I've heard people complain about the pre-trip wait time (it's recommended you get there an hour before your scheduled departure time). But terminals on both sides of the water now have eateries and shopping where you can nosh, browse, and even enjoy a drink or two (as long as you're not driving) before your voyage. The Cape May terminal is a great spot to enjoy a sunset, too, and it's home to the festivals run by the Garden State Wine Growers Association. Again—only if you're not driving. No need to add DUI to your trip.

One more tip: make sure to bring a valid photo ID and your passport if you're not a U.S. citizen.

themed show or two, from the classic Scrooge tale to *Every Christmas Story Ever Told*, which zips through holiday traditions in one sitting. $$.

Important Info

Where to turn when you need to know

EMERGENCY NUMBERS

In an emergency, dial 911.
Poison information: 800-222-1222.
Non-emergency police: 609-463-6570.

HOSPITALS

Cape Regional Medical Center (609-463-2000; caperegional.com), 2 Stone Harbor Blvd., Cape May Courthouse 08210.

The end   Courtesy of Marc Steiner/Agency New Jersey

NEWSPAPERS

Cape May County Herald (609-886-8600; capemaycountyherald.com).
Exit Zero (609-898-9874; exitzero.us).

REALTORS

Coastline Realty (800-377-7843; coastlinerealty.com), 1400 Texas Ave.,
Cape May 08204.
Jersey Cape Realty (800-643-0043; jerseycaperealty.com), 739 Washington
St., Cape May 08204.
Wilsey Realty (609-884-1007; wilseyrealty.com), 501 Lafayette St., Cape
May 08204.

TRANSPORTATION

Aart's Cape May Taxi (609-898-7433; capemaytaxi.com).
High Roller Transportation (609-425-5819).

TOURISM CONTACTS

Greater Cape May Chamber of Commerce (609-884-5598; capemay
chamber.com).
Mid-Atlantic Center for the Arts & Humanities (800-275-4278; cape
maymac.org).
New Jersey Travel and Tourism (800-VISITNJ; state.nj.us/travel).

Index